Around the script in 80 secrets

By
Laura de los Santos

Around the script in 80 secrets
ISBN: 9781706541066
Copyright © 2019 - Laura de los Santos
laudelos@outlook.com
https://www.linkedin.com/in/lauguionista/

All rights reserved. This book or any portion thereof may not be reproduced or used in any manner whatsoever without the express written permission of the author except for the use of brief quotations in a book review.

Original Title: La vuelta al guion en 80 secretos
ISBN: 978-950-895-294-3
© 2010

Translation by: Paola L. Jarast
paolaluciajarast@gmail.com

For Val,

whose miraculous persistence
opened the Vatican's front gate.

Because of you, I'll never give up.

Index

Introduction 9
Theater, TV, Internet, and Movies 11

   1. The Specific Characteristics of the Theater Script 12
   2. The Specific Characteristics of the TV Script 15
   3. The Specific Characteristics of the Internet Script 18
   4. The Specific Characteristics of the Movie Script 20

Scripts according to their duration 23

   5. Short film (up to 30 minutes of duration) 24
   6. Medium-length films (between 30 and 80 minutes) 27
   7. Feature film (more than 80 minutes) 29

Adaptations 31

   8. From theater to the big screen 32
   9. From literature to the big screen 35
   10. From the big screen to the big screen 39

The Characters 43

   11. Define your characters and their interrelationships 43
   12. Zodiac signs and Chinese horoscope 46
   13. Fall in love with ALL your characters 48
   14. Awareness of desire vs. Desire of awareness 50
   15. What are the objectives? 53
   16. Given circumstances 55
   17. The body is a consequence of the state of mind 57
   18. They must undergo a transformation throughout the story 59

The dialogues 61

   19. Writing dialogues is like playing chess against oneself 61
   20. How do the characters speak? 64
   21. Explanation in dialogues is boring 66
   22. Eternal monologues are almost always failures 69
   23. Start your dialogues in the middle of the action and avoid fillers ... 71

The Scenarios 73

   24. The place must be another character 73
   25. Why THIS place and not any other? 76
   26. Common scenarios 77

27. Visit the scenarios that you have in mind. By day, by night. Each place has unique qualities. You will come up with ideas..........79

The Wildcards 81

28. Characters and/or objects that seem to have nothing to do with the story 81
29. Plot outline..........83
30. The treatment 85
31. Ellipsis..........86
32. The flashback..........88
33. The flashforward 90
34. The voice-over..........92
35. The hateful signs that indicate temporality..........94
36. Do not start a script thinking about the genre. Build a structure and adapt it to the genre you want later. 95
37. Sit in a bar to listen to people's conversations 96
38. Watch all the movies that relate to your idea 97

Rarely considered details 99

39. The average viewer of your story..........99
40. Reality exceeds fiction by far 101
41. Do not fall in love with a shot or idea 103
42. 'This is a bad idea; it has already been done' is not always so. An original twist can become a new story. 104
43. Be careful with the timing of your story. Consider the average time of writing: a year. The average time of production: another year. And the average time till the premiere: another year. Three years from your original idea. 105

Comments that promise failures..........107

44. 'What if I take this short that won three awards and make it a feature?'..........107
45. 'Last night I had a great dream. I'm going to write a script.'..........109

General Genres..........111

46. The Love Story 112
47. The most common flaws in the love story 114
48. Action movies..........115
49. The most common flaws in action movies..........117
50. The adventure 118
51. The most common flaws in adventure..........120
52. The Suspense 121
53. The most common flaws in suspense 123

54. The Horror	124
55. The most common flaws in horror films	126
56. Science fiction	127
57. The most common flaws in science fiction	129
58. The Fantastic	130
59. The most common flaws in the fantastic	133
60. Crime and investigation	134
61. The most common flaws in crime and investigation stories	136
62. The Comedy	137
63. The most common flaws in comedy	140
64. The documentary	141
65. The most common flaws in the documentary	143

My mind is blank! 145

I don't know how to start 146

66. Nothing begins. Everything is *In Media Res* 146
67. Obliged questions of the spectator (none must be answered immediately) 148
68. Recreation: A good chocolate cake with a banana smoothie 149

I don't know how to go forward with the story 150

69. Small successive conflicts 150
70. The 15-minute crisis 151
71. The 30-minute crisis 153
72. The 60-minute crisis 154
73. Annoying questions (because they force you to check the entire text) ... 156
74. Recreation: A bicycle ride 158

I don't know how to finish 159

75. The 90-minute crisis 159
76. The Anticlimax 160

The Commercial vs. The Artistic 161

77. The commercial is not always a betrayal of art. Making money with talent can bring happiness 161
78. The love story does not promise a success; nor does the horror genre promise a failure 163
79. Timeless stories are more likely to become classics 165
80. That script under hire can give you the money to dedicate to that other one you want to write. Love it too. 166

Recommended Bibliography 169

Introduction

Welcome to this fascinating journey around the script. Thank you for being brave enough to find your way here, even if out of mere curiosity. Only the talented recognize what is strange as an opportunity to create something new. And if this book has made its way to your hands, it means not only that you belong in this category, but also that you're ready for a change in your life. And that is a good thing, because the purpose of this book is to be the humble servant of people like you, who don't settle and who know that there's much more to see than what is in front of your very nose.

The screenwriter's profession is sometimes hard and, more often than we would like, non-profitable. As screenwriters, we know that better than anyone. However, there are secrets, tools that you can use to extract from your talent something more than the pure pleasure derived from exploiting it. Within these pages, you'll find a lot of secrets that will make you renew the perspective of your own screenwriting. You will have unconditional support and a series of resources that you'll be able to carry with you wherever you go; they will never leave you, and they'll provide you with enough confidence so as to create not only a work of art, but also a product you'll proudly call 'worthy'.

At the end of every specific point (whenever possible) you will find examples of movies that will help you comprehend and better set the posed ideas. However, these examples are in no way considered to be the only ones nor the best ones. And the person writing these lines would like nothing more than for you to find your own examples, especially if they become the inspiration for future scripts. Bear in mind that the examples that serve as tools for us today, and are hailed as masterpieces, were at some point rough drafts as well. Be generous with your neighbor and allow him or her to count on your knowledge too.

Footnotes and asterisks will be avoided, so you don't end up turning this manual- which is supposed to be pragmatic- into a carousel; your brain must be providing you with enough inconveniences as it is.

Consider this introduction a warning, because once you finish reading the whole book, there will be no going back. A new turning point will arise in the script of your life, and it will be up to you to have enough courage to take the reins of the new experiences that you'll be confronted with. If, until now, as a writer, you thought that success was a matter of luck, remember that from this moment on, it will be just another situation in life you'll have to learn to deal with. Are you ready to get on this train? Do you think you are brave enough to face a new life, filled with mysteries and charms? If your answer is yes, then LET'S GO!

Theater, TV, Internet, and Movies

When an idea pops into our minds, one of the first things we need to do is... write it down!!! Because chances are, we're not going to be in the ideal place to develop it. A lot of screenwriters go through life with recording devices to save an idea quickly. They carry said device everywhere, but when the perfect timing arrives and inspiration decides to make its appearance, the recorder has either gone missing, has ran out of batteries, or has simply decided to stop working.

In a nutshell, ideas are elusive. They appear suddenly, without seeking permission, and with the same nerve, they go away. If we are lucky enough to jot them down in something less ephemeral than our memory, we'll be able to work on them later, when we finally sit before the computer.

Writing under request has some characteristics that favor it, different from those scripts that take shape just because. They already have an assigned theme, a means of exhibition, and a specific duration. That's why we're *not* going to deal with them in this book. We're going to explore the other ones, the difficult and whimsical ones.

When we sit in front of the computer to begin with a new script, one of the first things we have to consider is the most convenient *means* of exhibition for it. As far as scripts are concerned, there are *four possible* ones. These are *theatre, television Internet,* and *movie*. Whereas it's true that in most cases the four can be interchangeable through adaptation, there's always one that suits our idea better. And if we haven't received an offer or signed a contract anyway, the smartest thing to do is to consider the best means of exhibition for it. Let's see.

1. The Specific Characteristics of the Theater Script

Theater is the oldest audiovisual means of them all. And it comes from afar. Ever since man felt the need to tell stories, he invented the means to be able to do it. Theater has the unique characteristic of presenting only *one* scenario and *one* point of view -the one of the spectator sitting in his chair, pretty far from the action, no matter how lucky he was to get a ticket in the first row. Theater needs its actors more than the other means. And this is due to the fact that they are basically everything it has. Yes, sure... the stage design does help. But the stage design on its own does not boost an entire play, while more than once, plays have been performed with nothing but actors, without even so much as a curtain- and successfully so.

The fact that the actor is so important, and that the spectator cannot get nearer to the action, compels the play to base its dramatic action in the dialogue and/or monologue; i.e., in *words*. In fact, this is the only means where it's credible for an actor to speak to himself. Speech in theater is a lot more than what it seems -it reflects a character's *actions* and *thoughts*. Let's see how:

- *Actions through words:*

On stage, any action which entails detail is useless. The spectator will never see it. Maybe the lucky one in the first row, but from there going backwards, spectators will miss most of it. It is well known that the theater actor performs for the ones in the last row. And if he wants to show his anger through action, he will probably have to plant a bomb and blow up half the stage. Not a very good idea for the second day of show, though. However, if he expresses himself through speech, with a good projection of his voice or a simple microphone, even the one in the very last row will be satisfied. This doesn't mean that a writer should get all excited and say, '*Ok. Then I'll write theater and I'll only have to worry about dialogue*'. Because when dialogue is *the only thing you have*, expressing everything in an appealing manner counting on this *and only this is* not as simple as it may seem.

Characters' actions in theater are well marked on stage. They must be in place 'X', when they say line 'Y'. This is due to the fact that anything that stresses words is very welcomed and thanked. When one has to tell a story and all he has are words, the thousands and even millions of terms in a language are always few. Everything revolves around speech and the rest is only useful to renew what is said.

- *Thoughts through words:*

The universe of thoughts is something that's usually saved for literary novels and written stories, and for theater. They are used in every means, but in cinema and television, to express thoughts through words is like taking advantage of a parking lot for the handicapped just because it turns out to be useful since it's near the access door. In other words, these two means have unique tools which are a lot more interesting than just saying, 'I'm sad as the sea in a rainy day'. Theater, on the other hand, is closer to written work. That is the reason why theater plays are commonly published as books. As was said before, in theater, speech is everything. If we want to express sadness through a tear running down someone's cheek, we are on the wrong track. Once again, the spectator in the last row will bother his neighbor, asking for explanations; to no avail, of course, because he'll be drowning in the same waters. Let's imagine then what will happen when we try to explain to the audience what a character *is up to*; when we try to convey what he's thinking through a table on stage full of lots of messed up papers. Oh, yeah... there will be a lot more than two spectators frowning, a question mark on their faces.

Thoughts transmitted through words in theater are not a tool, they are a *necessity*. Sadly, habit makes spectators accept this tool in cinema and television a lot more than they should. And screenwriters take advantage of this convenience.

But there's no need to panic. We will delve into the *other* resources that film and TV have to offer.

What you must have in mind as a screenwriter is where your talent is headed. There are some people for whom it's very simple to tell a story through dialogue, and they should definitely stick to theater. Others find solace in the expression of feelings through images, and they should therefore stick to cinema. And we also have the TV talents, who are able to connect twenty characters through a universe of confusion and entanglement, which they then manage to maintain throughout fifty episodes.

The purpose of this book is help you express yourself in the most comfortable way possible. That's why we insist on the fact that every story has a means that is better suited to it.

Examples of theater plays that make great use of speech are:

- It's not always good to exaggerate, but it won't be far from the truth to state that *all* of Shakespeare's work is worthy of consideration. This little man from the XVI Century has done such a great task transmitting human emotions and thoughts through monologue and dialogue that to this day his work is not outmoded.
- But, anyway, if we're looking for something more recent, one great play is *'Trees Die Standing Tall'*, by Alejandro Casona. The interesting thing about this play (in this particular case, anyway, because it's perfect, from beginning to end) is how characters use speech to talk about what cannot be said: a secret. To use concepts to express exactly the opposite of what would be expected to achieve with them is more often than not a great idea.
- One more example: musicals. Cinema has done wonders with musicals, but to see a person, or rather, *many people*, using their vocal chords, live, is an opportunity that no one should miss out, because it's an excellent way of conveying both feeling and thoughts at the same time through speech. Plays worth watching are:
- *'Les Misérables'*, by Claude-Michel Schönberg (composer) and Alain Boublil (script), from 1980, based on the homonymous novel by Victor Hugo;
- *'The Phantom of the Opera'*, by Andrew Lloyd Webber, from 1986, based on the book by Gaston Leroux;
- *'Dracula, the musical'*, script by Pepe Cibrian and music by Christian Mahler, from 1991, based on the homonymous novel by Bram Stoker.

2. The Specific Characteristics of the TV Script

As anticipated above, television displays characteristics that make it unique in its style. Because TV is filmed, we can afford to show details that are impossible in theater. But on TV there is a new problem: *time*. Yes, TIME. On television, there is *no time* for anything. Everyone is always on the run, and usually tomorrow's episode is being written while the one that was written yesterday is being filmed. Television has a basic problem that has to do with the spectator. Unlike the cinema or the theater, TV has *competition*. Imagine our friendly viewer sitting comfortably at home with his feet up on the coffee table and the lovely *remote control* in his hand. Not to mention that there used to be a time where there were only a few channels and you pressed the little button a couple of times and quickly got back to where you had started. Today, channel surfing has become an art that even the younger ones master, and one has more than 200 channels to choose entertainment from. That we get the audience to pause that little frantic finger on our program is an art that only a couple of people master. But how will all this affect the script for television? Let's see.

While virtually everything on television has a script, even a basic one, we will only deal with fiction scripts. Say, soap operas, sitcoms, and others with daily or weekly runs. Beyond the specific characteristics of each genre (which will be detailed later in the book), there is something shared by all TV scripts, which relates to these little problems mentioned above:

Just as television has nightmares about channel surfing, its main food is *advertising*, which is basically the principal reason why one takes its finger back to the remote control. The ad space on TV is essential, because otherwise no one would eat. So, you should always consider the commercial breaks and leave the viewer on the edge of his seat so that he is so hooked that he forgets about the remote control. Ok. That would be a miracle. But we can try. The best way to get someone to keep his attention focused on our program is that all sort of things happen all the time. So, it's best to create a dozen characters that are interrelated in the most scandalous possible way. Or funny; funny things also hold the viewer's attention.

In cinema or theater, we can afford to have peaks of tension interspersed with explanatory moments, which are perhaps boring. Our audience is not going to leave the room to get into the neighboring function in a sort of sports zapping. He paid for his ticket and will be left to endure whatever we have to show him. Except, of course, in cases where the viewer decides to leave the room to avoid a resounding attack of drowsiness. But for that purpose, these words and you are gathered here; so that when you sit down to write the next time, you don't panic. These lines will try to offer you as many tools as possible to go into battle well-equipped and with at least one strategy.

Resuming the topic of the velocity of television, where time is money and where attention is everything, we suggest that those who have an idea in which the most important things are characters and their interrelationships consider devoting themselves to television. Mostly because movies, in general, have the limit of two to three hours, and it's possible that we will be unable to develop all the characters, and some stories will inevitably remain open-ended; and theater has its space limited to a single stage, and it will be impossible for the spectator in the last row to understand who's who, especially considering that we cannot keep the viewer interested for fifty minutes of verbal introduction of characters.

Another characteristic that also favors television is that if we are successful, the producer will want to continue our series for several more seasons, and having many characters is the best way to stretch a story.

Examples:

- The first case is invariably the series '*Lost*', created by JJ Abrams, Jeffrey Lieber and Damon Lindelof. The series ran for six seasons between 2004 and 2010. For the writers of the various episodes credit, it is more practical to use the Internet:
http://www.imdb.com/title/tt0411008/fullcredits#writers

This TV series has such an effective work on characters and relationships that one actually remains on the edge of the seat all the time, hooked on the successive conflicts.

- The second case is the sitcom *'Friends'*, by creators David Crane and Marta Kauffman. It ran for ten seasons between 1994 and 2004. The list of writers is, once again, too large to reproduce. Best: http://www.imdb.com/title/tt0108778/fullcredits#writers

In this case, there aren't many characters, only six –three women and three men. But every one of them has such unique traits that they achieve the purpose of keeping the audience hooked while they learn about the various entanglements and conflicts the characters get into.

3. The Specific Characteristics of the Internet Script

Although the Internet has already invaded every aspect of our lives in a massive, totally disrespectful way, there is still a lot to say about the scripts that will end up running through this channel.

I'm going to separate these scripts in a pragmatic way:

- The time we spend submerged in our phone/tablet.
- The time we spend in front of the TV watching VOD content.

Both of these are consuming more and more of our time each day, which, as screenwriters is... of course... GREAT!! A lot more content to be made fast! Watching content through the Internet has all the benefits TV has without the disgusting advertising. It truly suits our demands. So, we don't necessarily have to leave our spectator on the edge of the seat. BUT! We still have to create interesting content. So, in that way, all the secrets you'll find here will serve you well.

The main difference between watching something in a theater or a TV or a cell phone is the size of the screen. It is obvious, I know. But when it comes to shooting a movie or a series, it doesn't look so obvious. When we shoot content that is mainly thought for cell phones, we must certainly forget about huge landscapes and earthly catastrophes, because they will not transmit the desired effect to the spectator. Also, they are usually very expensive. Another reason NOT to think of them.

One more thing that has more to do with the director than the screenwriter that I don't recommend doing in this kind of audiovisuals are quick pans, camera shakings, and important objects that are placed somewhere at the back of the stage, away from the action going on in the front. When you write and shoot for cell phones, the best advice I can give you is to consider your spectator as someone on a bus going at full speed in the middle of traffic. You get the idea, right?

Going back to the specifics of screenwriting for cell phones, the stories are and usually should be short. Say something to the audience in no more than 2 to 5 minutes. And if you want to say more, split it in tiny episodes of that duration. This is the best way to keep the audience engaged in these fast-moving times.

VOD for TV, on the other hand, offers a lot more space for creativity. As it has been said, you can have the TV benefits without the ads, and TVs are getting bigger and smarter, with amazing quality and detail. BUT! (oh yeah, there's always a but) But... that definitely DOES NOT give us the power to create lousy content. Creative, rich, inspiring content is always first and foremost. So, thank God you are reading this book now!

With VOD content, we don't have channel surfing as we know it, but spectators can easily press stop and look for something different to watch. No matter how much money they spent on that specific rent or purchase or the money they pay monthly to VOD companies, we should always show them respect them with great quality content.

TV series are in fashion these days, and fashion is always easier to get sponsored. But I still recommend that you write what you know and what you feel comfortable about if you don't have a specific contract yet. Consider what you find easier to write about and come back to these words for the best exhibition means for it.

4. The Specific Characteristics of the Movie Script

If theater is action through words, and television is action... say... period, cinema is known for its action through *image*. In this category we can also include action through *sound*. Not sounds of dialogue, but all other sounds: music, noises, environments, whether they are coming or not from the field of dramatic action. Most of the movies, at least commercial ones, have a significant amount of dialogue. The fact is that a film is always more bearable when we hear the characters speak. This has to do with a mere matter of habit, which is closely related also to theater and television. Some lines of dialogue collaborate in the development of the action. The problem is that we often lose sight of the boundary between image and dialogue, and when we look back to our script, we are dealing with an audio-visual stuttering, where characters speak about things that we're already seeing onscreen.

Cinema has plenty of tools that are unique. In movies, we can give the details as much attention as we wish. We can see a tear, a cat scratch, a small scar. The detail in a film says it all. Even the environmental details: a striped vase, a face in a picture, a drop of coffee on the imported sofa. The film has the potential to offer as many points of view as we want. And occasions where the perfect shot refuses to make itself known are rare. In cinema, the image offers hundreds of conflicts of interest; they only need a moment to explain themselves. Therefore, it is important to take into account the type of idea that we develop. As already mentioned, if most of the action happens inside the character's mind, it will be best for us to spend some quality time reading Shakespeare and then dive into an exciting play, so we don't have to suffer with unrealistic monologues in movies or television.

On the other hand, in cinema, it's impossible to keep a spectator stressed for long. He will not resist it and eventually his attention will diminish. Therefore, it is essential to intersperse tension with calm. But calm on television is provided by advertising, so our program must contain action almost 100% of the time. If you're one of those writers who always find a problem in every situation, and feel that your idea is a relentless conflict, consider writing TV series. This does not mean, of course, that the idea cannot be developed in any of the other media. The intention here is not to add restrictions to talent, but to take an idea towards the most suitable means.

In this opportunity, only the world of screenwriting will be researched, due to the simple fact that this book is not meant to be an encyclopedia, but a *vademecum*. Its purpose is to disclose most of the secrets that enable to work on any idea in a movie format. If you feel that although your idea would be better in the theater or on television, you need to explore the world of filmmaking, this book will help you achieve your goal. The intention is to provide the necessary tools for you to avoid panicking at the blank page and exploit your talents to the fullest while waiting for an offer to write a script under request.

It really isn't worth introducing examples here, because they will be explained in detail below. Furthermore, if we had to choose one example, any would be good. Beyond the different points of views that each spectator has, you only need to look at the long list of credits at the end of a movie to understand it took a huge effort to make it, and as a good filmmaker, you will surely be able to find *something* good in all of them. In this book, not a single name or surname will be mentioned and given a bad review. Effort itself deserves respect. Just think about the simple fact that the makers of *that* movie that you don't like are already one step ahead of us in terms of experience and, as such, they deserve to be recognized. Moreover, when some filmmakers are explicitly mentioned, it will only be with the modest aim of paying tribute to the inexhaustible talent running through the projector, inspiring us to be more creative and better filmmakers.

Scripts according to their duration

When we think of writing a script, another issue to consider is the *duration* (always in the case of a script based on your own idea, of course, not one written under request). Because according to the type of conflict and its length, it will be better for us to choose one of the three formats below. One isn't really better than the other; today there are so many festivals for shorts (maybe less for medium-length films), as there are for feature films. And, with the appearance of VOD, we can also make one-hour movies that will now find their way towards spectators. Movies, throughout History, have always worked like a pendulum between independents and studios. At first, there were a few who made films separately, and when they began to succeed, they came together to form more important production companies, with the possibility of investing more money in films. The good thing was that they started to reach a bigger audience. The bad thing was that only a few decided what was being filmed and what not. With that, before long, the films became repetitive and trite. The spectator then went to look for new ideas and relied more on independent films. That's how small films (small in terms of monetary investment, not in terms of quality) began to make themselves known, and once again the film industry opened. But with this newfound fame of the renovated filmmakers came new possibilities to grow into production companies. And so on and so on.

At present, we are at that moment when the spectator is tired once more of the great productions and again goes in search of original things to watch. And with the advent of Internet technology, it is much easier to promote the works of short duration. So, these little films are all the rage now. Not to mention, of course, that it is much more accessible for independents to work in a short or medium-length film than in a feature, for obvious monetary reasons. So, it is no less relevant to go over the characteristics of these two formats as well as the feature film.

5. Short film (up to 30 minutes of duration)

The fundamental characteristics of the short films are two:

- *Start right in the middle of the conflict*

This is because there is no time for an introduction of main characters, much less for the secondary ones; we don't even have time to introduce a scenario. Only the introduction of the conflict, plus its development and its subsequent resolution, will cover all the time. As shots begin to stretch, or become very explanatory, we will be exceeding our time. That's not a bad thing, but in general, the main motivation for writing a short film is a tempting contest or festival. The short film is written almost in a couple of hours, and contests usually come with an assigned theme and also a limited *duration*. The organizers of these festivals can be very strict as regards following the guidelines; they use this as a filter for the large amount of material they receive. And the idea is that you, who are reading these lines now, are not left out of a competition owing to something as trivial as that. To avoid wasting time with annoying disappointment after having already put in time in writing, be warned that if it gets very descriptive or explanatory, and if you start introducing the characters instead of putting them directly in a conflict, you will probably exceed time. Start out directly with the crash, or explosion, or the accidental encounter, or the phone call, or the scream after the nightmare. From the first line, the script has to burst. Whoever reads it should be hooked immediately. That will have made your time worthwhile, and at least your material will be read in the contest or festival.

- *A twist at the end*

The end of any work involves 75% of the personal opinion of whoever reads your screenplay. If the judge of the competition likes your short from the start (because you managed to hook him with an immediate conflict), but when he reaches the end, the resolution is poor, he'll probably discard your material on account of his disappointment. Imagine... Mr. Judge is fascinated with what he has in his hands. After reading a ton of boring stuff, full of explanations, he sighs and opens a new script, your script, the one you created with so much effort after feeling inspired with these lines. And he reads and reads looking forward to that grand finale, while feeling a duality, because for the first time he's reading something interesting and does not want it to end. But the script has already submitted its dispute and is galloping towards the end. And then... plaff! It was all a dream, and someone gets up, stumbling, still with a powerful hangover, and facing the bathroom mirror says, '*I just had the craziest dream...*'

Please... do yourself a favor and try to avoid that kind of ending. That is NOT a twist. That is what happens when you do not know how to finish your story. The turn of the screw is *implicit in the initial conflict*. And, in general, has to do with the *contrary* reaction that the conflict is supposed to provoke. That means: after an action, there is always a reaction that is usually expected, right? 'Face of shock' after a loud and inexplicable noise, 'crying' after bad news, etc... If we think about the opposite of that reaction, which is, 'laughter' after a loud noise, or 'joy' after bad news, but we reserve that emotion for the end of the short, we will be creating a twist. And the most interesting thing is that it will always be connected with the rest of the story, because it *derived from it* in the beginning. Finding out how bad news can generate joy depends on the talent of every writer. The simple answer to that question will immediately lead you to sit in front of the computer.

We must play with the information we provide the spectator with from the beginning of the film. That is, we must *make him believe* that something is happening, while something else is *actually* happening that we will disclose at the end. Let's take an example:

We know that John is sad now, and we know he will be laughing at the end. What the spectator does not know is that John was *never really* sad; he only *acted* as such to reach his goal. The spectator will see that John is sad, but we as writers will know that this is a lie to trick him, to drive him progressively towards the joy at the end. But it is also necessary to place *signs* along the story for the spectator to logically understand then that the character was *never* sad. These signs may be: a diary in which John writes his deeds, which may seem like something the character does on account of nostalgia, a small but sudden move when another character approaches, which can go undetected with a sudden noise, etc...

What is absolutely essential is that you, as a writer, know what turn you are going to give to your story *from the beginning*. That way you can play with the viewer, give him little signs that he will be able to connect only when you reveal the truth of the facts *at the end*. Then the judge of the contest will be delighted.

A general characteristic of short films is also a limitation on the number of characters, which must all be main characters. In a short there's no time for secondary ones. There are always exceptions, of course, but generally one fails to develop them sufficiently, because there is no time for subplots or side stories. If we see that our idea can extend longer than a short film, because we have another interesting subplot, we should seriously consider the option of working on a medium-length film. Forcing the stories to fit in less time than you need to explain things, leads inevitably to misunderstanding.

Examples:

- *'The 56'*, by Lucrecia Martel, 1988.
- *'For the Birds'*, by Ralph Eggleston, 2000.
- *'The Glove'*, by Juan Pablo Zaramella, 2003.
- *'Company'*, by Álex Hernández, 2006.
- *'Dustin'*, by Kristina Jaeger, 2015.

6. Medium-length films (between 30 and 80 minutes)

Mid-length is a format that is relatively less worked on in cinema because of the channels of exhibition it has to deal with. It's always short for a feature film that could be projected in a theater, and it's always long to be exploited through the Internet, because it's usually too heavy. Mid-length is usually used for TV in documentaries or series. This format is more likely to be seen in festivals, which unfortunately shorten the possibilities of massive exhibitions. But all these things don't make this format less interesting. There are films that last two to three hours, which could well be perfectly narrated in one hour alone, in a neater manner. What happens is that the writers know that this format is not the most advisable to make money, and when they see they have an idea that does not fit into a short film, they immediately go for the feature film. And then the film is stretched like gum, full of downtime and cumbersome verbal explanations of things we are already understanding with the images. Before you spend so many hours sitting at the computer, or worse, at the... typewriter! Note that the mid-length film is a format as possible and perhaps as interesting as the others.

The mid-length film offers some more possibilities that the short film. It gives us the possibility of a short -yes... *short*- introduction to the characters before launching into the central conflict. It also gives us the opportunity to work on one or two -I said... *one or two*- secondary conflicts. Ideally, the secondary conflict should be in direct relation to the main plot, and if they are opposed, all the better. That way, the spectator will have at least two points of view of the same situation and feel included in the story, identified. This is what you want as a writer: for the spectator to be attracted to your story. And to offer at least two points of view is an infallible way to accomplish that.

Of course, the turn of the screw serves in this format and the feature film as well. The thing is that it is much harder to achieve. But if we take a short film contest for practice, we can master this little happy secret and leave the audience with a final surprise, the cherry on top of the ice cream. It is more difficult because, as mentioned above, the twist has to be introduced from the *beginning of the conflict*, and we have *one* conflict *only* in the short film. From the mid-length film onwards, the plot is a sum of small obstacles to overcome, to which were add small optional secondary conflicts. That means more actions to take into account and more unexpected reactions to control for effective twists.

But do not despair, dear screenwriter, because I am not going to present a problem if you are not offered at least one solution. Difficult does not mean impossible; it just requires more effort. So, what I recommend in case of working on the final surprise, is that you *put down on paper the reactions that the initial conflicts of your script provoke*. Remember you *must know the ending* when you begin typing, to take the twist forward effectively. So, from the first reactions in your characters, consider how to turn them into the *opposite* at the end. Bearing these ideas in mind, you can work on the different emotions in your characters so that the spectator thinks about what you want him to think.

For examples of medium length films, basically the whole documentary programming of the Discovery Channel and the History Channel are worth your while. They never last more than one hour, and although you may not believe it, they have a beginning, middle and end. They even bother to always leave some itching in the middle, because, remember this is TV and the commercial breaks are vital.

Usually, these documentaries respect the characteristic mentioned above -some secondary characters who contribute to the central story or conflict with their testimony. You only have to sit for a while in front of the TV to not only study the scripts of these medium-length films, but also to take the opportunity to enrich a bit.

Another way to exploit these types of stories are the TV series that present different stories in every chapter, all intertwined by a particular theme. The best example I can think of is *Black Mirror*, created by Charlie Brooker. For writing credits, you can check:

http://www.imdb.com/title/tt2085059/fullcredits?ref_=tt_cl_sm#cast

This kind of stories are also in fashion in these internet and VOD times.

7. Feature film (more than 80 minutes)

At this point, it seems that the feature film offers all the possibilities that in short and medium length films are limitations. We can have all the characters we want (keeping in mind that not every one of them will be main characters and that the more characters we have, the harder it will be to close all their stories), we can add a good number of subplots, which offers several different points of view, and we can even work to create all kind of scenarios. Time is on our side. Even if we realize that our story is too long, we can split the film in part I and part II. The film offers endless possibilities that can be exploited successfully. And throughout this book we will work on a good amount of them.

BUT... (there's always a 'but') just as the infinite possibilities can be very inspiring, not having any limitations may be distressing, because you won't have any parameter. And that's not always a good idea. So, it is best to establish the parameters beforehand ourselves. And a good way to do it is to select what *format* or *duration* suits us better; then, the number of characters and conflicts we should have, which of them weigh more, which we should discard, which we had not previously thought about, etc., will come immediately to our mind. These questions set the first limits that will serve as floor to our precious structure. And if we also ask ourselves *which means of exhibition* is best suited to our idea, we will realize that, unintentionally, we already have a lot to begin to work on. And just that is a huge breakthrough. At least we will not be staring at a blank page, knowing that we have to write if we want to succeed, but with our mind so blocked by the endless possibilities that we end up panicking.

The feature film is by far the most difficult of the three formats, especially because our treacherous ability to *remember* comes in to play. Memory is a critical factor in the feature film script and you're probably going to have to reread what you write many times, especially after page #30. Because the issue is this: every writer has a different way to express themselves, and when one is immersed in the writing, talent shines through and shows its own style without asking for permission. If, when reaching the middle of the script, we forget the descriptions or dialogues of the first sheets -which will undoubtedly happen if we don't reread constantly-, we will become repetitive and we'll discover that there are several characters expressing themselves in the same way, we'll describe details thinking it's the first time we do it when in fact we've already done that pages ago, etc. Those mistakes will stay in the spectator's mind, as he will find those repetitions familiar. They make him uncomfortable. And you don't want *that* to happen, dear screenwriter, do you? The bitter taste you leave in the spectator's mouth will come out when he comments *your* film with his friends. So, please, don't forget to *reread* what you write constantly.

Of course, there are many details that must be taken into account, but we will work on them throughout the book in an orderly manner, so you know which ones are most important regarding your idea. The intention here is to collaborate with the making of great writers and you know you can be one of them. If not, you simply wouldn't be reading this now. So, have faith in yourself and feed your talent.

These first six points, as you can verify if you sit down to write without reading further, give us the opportunity to begin developing an idea from a *structural* point. What tends to happen when we have an idea is that our brain begins to work like crazy, thinking about a million things at once, without understanding any of them, and perhaps forgetting everything by the time we try the third pen, which is the one that finally releases ink on the paper.

Given these first secrets, we can train our brains to remember only the main idea without the fear of missing something when we finally have that blessed minute to jot it down on paper. Because just by thinking about the *means of exhibition* and *format*, we will be working in an orderly manner from the beginning, and we will know how many business opportunities our idea offers without even having made a storyboard. Interesting, right? Well, do not abandon your reading now. Continue this journey around the script and prove yourself that you can be much more than just an amateur tourist.

Adaptations

There are some issues that are common to all formats that were ever invented for storytelling. All of them have *characters*; they generally have a *line of dramatic action* that consists of a beginning, a middle and an end; they all have *certain scenarios*, etc. These issues are what make it possible for these formats to be *interchangeable*. This, however, does not mean that any story can be told *in the same way* in any format. It is essential to know the secrets and tricks of each to be able to go from one to another without tripping or failures. We have already mentioned theater, television and film, and now we'll add the literary form and reveal how alchemy occurs.

One of the main limitations that we *think* we have when we adapt an artwork is the *moment in History* in which the action takes place. And the truth is that we can play with it as much as with the amount of characters, the scenarios, etc. What we must keep untouched for it to be an adaptation are the work's *theme* and *central conflicts*. The more we play with the other tools, the most interesting the new work will be.

Adaptations are usually carried out under request, and in general it is a work that has been successful in its medium and some producer decided that if the work could succeed in one format, it could also do it in the form of a movie or TV series. For this reason, perhaps not *all*, but *almost* all the classics in theater and literature have been adapted for the big screen at some point; even the classic films have also had their chance to be *re*-worked on for the same medium. A bestseller's ink is still wet and voracious producers are already lurking around to transform it into a movie. And the truth is these money-minded men are not that mistaken when they imagine that the film will be a box office success. The problem is that they imagine it for the *wrong reasons*. These films are usually seen by more people than any other because they already carry *advertising* from the previous format, but it usually happens that the adaptation ceases to be an artwork and becomes an empty product. This is also because the producers want the work to be adapted with the highest fidelity possible, as close to the original format as possible, because they do not want to risk anything. This turns out to be a pitiful event because although we have a sure winner within our hands, we will not give the work the possibility to achieve that success *by itself*. But it is not this book's intention to do a thorough analysis of the scripts under request, for, although they are the ones that mean money every time, they are also the ones that most limit our creativity. Here you will be taught how to take a book and turn it into an *original adaptation* by itself.

8. From theater to the big screen

As it has been said before, theater has features which are *unique* and are interesting only *in this medium*. With this in mind, it often happens that the plays that become classics succeed because they have been able to exploit that medium to its maximum. This is the first problem we have to consider when adapting a play to a movie.

Theater is words turned into actions. And film is *images* turned into actions. To ensure that the film maintains its style with an idea that was initially designed for theater, we must *turn words into images*. That is, when we think about cinema, we have to take into account the *weight* that an image has. One word can make us think of endless images. If we ask each spectator in the cinema to imagine how a monologue from Hamlet could be filmed, we will see that one by one new and different ways to do it will emerge. So, when we finally select the one we think is best, we'll probably make one man happy, and the rest of those watching will become harsh critics. Most people imagine what they listen to as they want to, and if we have the work of a good playwright in our hands, which is probably the case, considering that we are talking about a hit, it will have played so well with the mind of our audience that it'll have shown them the least possible and *told* them the rest, for them to *imagine* it as they please, because that's what works in theater. But we do not want to do filmed theater. We want to make movies. So, if we get a play and just rewrite it in film format, we will be making a big mistake: *we will bore* our creativity almost as much as the audience.

Let us return to what was mentioned above about the temporality of History. Let us suppose that our play takes place in 1763. At that time, people spoke in a particular way, dressed in a particular way, and acted in a particular way. As all of us writers know, there are *themes* in the works that are always eternal. Examples: Love, hate, revenge, lust, innocence, etc., etc. If we analyze the theme(s) of the work that we intend to adapt and put them in a bag together with our main conflict (also the secondary ones, if we want) and throw them into a time machine, we can have a story told in a thousand different ways, all interesting, on the big screen. If, on the other hand, we leave the story in its time, we will not be innovating much, because everything visual that that work has will already be present in the theater. One of the most interesting messages that we transmit when we move a story to any part of the time, is that Humanity *has not changed much* since the beginning of time. We believe that we evolve continuously, and yet the *themes* are repeated over and over again. That is why we can put in the skin of a postmodern adolescent a conflict that the author thought for a woman in her mid-thirties in the 1500. That way, we can carry forward the same conflicts and maintain the central theme of the work in a film completely different, totally visually enriched. The mere fact of thinking that we are not in ancient times but in the present time will make us discard scenarios, modify characters and renew lines of dialogues. And if we consider that every new thing that we add is going to be thought for the cinema, we will have a final product as good as the original, magically transformed.

To exemplify about theater transferred to film, we will use a strange case; strange in the sense that, in reality, this author did not write theater but literature. But her way of writing, with so few scenery and characters that talk about what they think and feel, enabled almost all her work to be adapted to theater at some point without any inconvenience. Ladies and gentlemen, I give you: Jane Austen. When we read one of her works, we instantly imagine ourselves in a seat in front of a stage. Her stories are always realistic, human and lacking in special effects. The scenarios, in general interiors of large houses -libraries, dining rooms, living rooms or bedrooms- or parks and forests, are always the same, easily adaptable to theater. The interesting thing to rescue here, when being transferred to cinema, are two cases in particular:

- The first is: *'Pride and Prejudice'*, from 1813. It has several adaptations for the big screen, but the one that concerns us this time is *'Bridget Jones' Diary'*, 2001. The person responsible for that script is Helen Fielding, who curiously had also written the homonymous novel before. And although the film bears more similarities with this novel than with Jane Austen's, the themes, conflicts and main characters have been maintained since the 19th century. The interesting thing to rescue here is the way they were precisely placed in a bag and released into a time machine. Because in the case of Bridget Jones, it is about a current woman; that is, hardworking and independent; a journalist who tries to survive in the madness of postmodernity. But, when thinking about men, she has the same doubts as Elizabeth Bennet, the protagonist of Jane Austen's work. She does not know if her love is going to be reciprocated, she is too proud to accept the love of a man she does not consider noble, she gets into the classic entanglements of prejudice and makes a mistake, believing that she has found her true love in the person who is actually lying to her. The update of this work meant that it was deliberatively enriched, and thus, the specific resources and tools available to each format could be used in each case.

- The second example is the play *'Emma'*, from 1815. Another very theatrical novel that had at least two period adaptations for cinema. But what interests us here is none of them, but *'Clueless'*, 1995, written by Amy Heckerling. With a powerful development of creativity, this woman succeeded in temporarily offsetting Austen's work. The characters, conflicts and themes remain perfectly as all the elements of modernity and the characteristics of the millionaire life in Beverly Hills are introduced in this new version, which is another reliable proof that it is not necessary for these issues to remain as though set in stone. As long as we maintain the basic characteristics of the characters and their interrelations, in addition to the conflicts and central themes, time and place can be perfectly expendable.

9. From literature to the big screen

Literature, on the other hand, presents a problem with which it is much more difficult to work in cinema than in any other format. That is: *thoughts*. All characters in literature have their minds open to the reader –or as much as the author wants, of course. The point is that we are dealing with something that has nothing to do with visual images; it's something so abstract that, to this day, the voice-over is still used to escape this nightmare. There are works of literature that are so much in the mind of a character that they become almost entirely descriptive. And when you read them, you imagine a lot of things visually that you think you can transfer to film without problems. These cases fail 95% of the times (the whereabouts of the other 5% are unknown, but the lucky ones must be somewhere hidden). Cinema *cannot get into the head of a character*. It must *show* what happens to him through its *actions* –or at least that is the interesting resource cinema has. The reality is that, thanks to voice-over, many movies have become filmed literature. Another serious mistake. Above all, because there is a myriad of tools with which the cinema counts, which the current viewer has decoded in an amazing way. Adapting a literary work that takes place in the mind of a character is a quick ticket to failure. Nothing like literature can tell a reader what a character is thinking without the help of dialogue. In literature, the character is '*devastated, corroded, amazed, in awe, in love*'. And with one word we have said everything. To demonstrate this in movies, we need at least a 2-minute scene for each emotion. Unless, of course, we apply the voice-over resource. But we will come back to this later.

We'll go crazy trying to adapt a work with characters who feel so much, but who act so little. However, many have tried, but they can never really convey everything that the character feels. And if the novel is basically about this, the film will be shipwrecked in the attempt. That is why it is suggested that, when adapting a literary work, one should first analyze how much actual action is present in it and how much occurs *inside the mind* of a character. You will save a lot of sweat and, above all, a lot of valuable time.

On the other hand, here the little trick of the temporal offset will come in handy. Although in this case, any scenario is new at a visual level because it has not been shown previously, transferring the work overtime changes the ways the characters act, the scenarios, and so on. In this way, the visual resources come to light, and everything that, for the screenwriter, becomes visual, will be of great help when making movies.

Any action that provokes a reaction in the 1700s will be modified by a wide variety of factors at the present time: technology, noises, new customs. And each character will react based on the medium in which he is immersed. No need to think too much to imagine the infinite scenarios in which you can place a character, and the screenwriter will notice how interesting it is to experiment with their reactions according to each case. This way you can see that there are elements that can be interchangeable without modifying the subject or the conflict.

Another factor that must be taken into account when adapting literature is that time does not go by the same way on paper as it does in the image. Time in writing and time in film do not even bear a resemblance. That is why it is sometimes so difficult to calculate how long our film will last. For this, what we must do is analyze all the actions that occur in the written text and calculate how long it would take to transfer it to film.

In general, literature describes *small actions*, which are *mixed with thoughts*. An example might be: '*I had only walked two blocks when I realized his true nature.*' From this phrase, only the first part is real action. And how will we *show* the second part? Hopefully somehow better than through voice-over. But if we think of the phrase for a moment, we will realize that it has two different cinematic times. The first part contains the action, so it is easier to determine how long it can take us to film it. For the second part (discarding the voice-over), we will have to think about the possible actions the character can perform in order to allow the spectator to *visually understand* that he has realized something. Will he stand still and retrace his steps? Will he lie down and start crying, heartbroken? Will he take out a cell phone and dial a number frantically? Each of these actions has a different time. And the duration of our scene will depend on the one we choose. But we could also ask another question. Is it really *necessary* for the character to realize the true nature of the other character while *walking down the street*, or can he do it in the comfortable armchair of his house? Because if it is an interior, it will be easier to film than an exterior, and maybe I can show it in a way that helps me save time for another important action. Or maybe I can join this action with the other that says, '*the TV was on, and on the news, I saw the rain and realized it would not let me carry out my plan.*' Maybe my character can realize the other's true nature, *while* seeing that the rain will ruin his plan. Anyway... each case is unique, of course. But it is good to know that the scenarios and actions *can be perfectly interchangeable*, and we will still be respecting the original idea. And we will also know that we can *discard actions* as long as we show what is truly important at some point in the film.

The literature that has fewer problems when it comes to being adapted to cinema is, of course, the one that has *a lot* of action.

Examples:

- The complete saga of *'The Lord of the Rings'*, by J. R. R. Tolkien, 1955; adapted to the cinema by Fran Walsh, during the years 2001, 2002 and 2003.
- The complete saga of *'Harry Potter'* by J. K. Rowling, edited between 1997 and 2007; written for cinema by Steve Kloves – except for *'The Order of the Phoenix'*, which was written by Michael Goldemberg – between 2002 and 2009.
- *'The Da Vinci Code'*, by Dan Brown, 2003; adapted for cinema by Akiva Goldsman in 2006.

These novels have small drawbacks when it comes to adapting, all related to temporality and spaces. But each of the writers knew how to solve these circumstances by exchanging scenarios and showing the most important events and characters without the need of respecting the times and places present in literary texts. In general, secondary characters are also dispensed with and/or several of them are taken and simplified into only one, more interesting character. This is risky and does not work every time, but it does solve some of the classic problems of lack of time.

In conclusion, it is always important, when adapting, to keep in mind who the characters are, which are essential and which are not, what the main conflicts and issues are, in how many places the story is carried out, which are really necessary or interesting and which are not -because, in that case, the most convenient thing will be to move to some other more visually striking space. Remember that this is cinema, and in cinema, image is everything. And if, after doing this analysis, you observe that you have characters that think a lot but don´t act that much, know that you are going to be getting into a cumbersome field. Nobody can assures that you will fail in the attempt and it is always better to try, but do not get frustrated if you end up discovering that that novel is not so interesting when you think about it in cinematographic terms. As mentioned earlier, there is a reason for stories to succeed more in one format than in another. It is not impossible to exchange them, but the author chose *that one* in the first place for some reason.

10. From the big screen to the big screen

The adaptations within the same format, and more commonly in cinema, are known as *remakes*. Remake means 'redo'. But redoing does *not* mean *copying* the previous model. Filmmakers often believe that if they take a film, whatever it is, and remake it by tracing the shot, they will get the same reaction from the viewer. That is why the films that are generally chosen were big blockbusters at the time. What they do *not* consider is that the spectator is *not* the same as the one before. As with best-seller adaptations, these films have the characteristic of advertising themselves, so it's easier for them to become massive, but that does not mean they hold the *interest* they awoke in the viewer the first time. To adapt a cinematographic work by repeating the previous film frame by frame doesn't make any sense in artistic terms. And the worst of all is that it will probably not generate the same interest in the current viewer. The only things we will get are: a more modern copy, better quality and special effects, and new faces, probably some star of the moment. But that will be all, and it will be a shame, too. To make cinema implies an effort that only those of us on this side know. The spectator simply arrives with his drink and his popcorn, sits in front of the screen and waits for the film to end to say *it was great* or *it went by so fast* or, to the filmmaker's discontent, just *mmmmh...*

As terrible as the script of a movie can be, there are always millions of other interesting things to salvage from a film. But, of course... the viewer just wants someone to tell him a story and to do it right. The films that were big hits at the time were so almost entirely because they were *well told*. And when a filmmaker takes one of these films, he usually believes that since it has already conquered the viewer once, it will do so again *in the same way*. But that's not true. The spectator always looks for new things that motivate his interest. And if you show him what he already knows, he will not be happy. Plus, hundreds of hours of hundreds of people and hundreds of rolls of film material will be wasted. The truth is that the first thing that must be modified so that the film remains interesting, even if the same story is told, is the *script*. Which is why you have this book in your hands. Look at all the responsibility you have as a talented writer. The potential jobs of many people will depend on you. The *artistic* potentialities of hundreds of people will depend on you. The novelty of the material, however old it may be, will depend on you. But, hey! Don't jump out of the building! This book will reveal some secrets that will help you to remain calm.

When choosing a film to remake in cinema, the first thing we have to find out is *the reason why it was a success* at the time. Because, as was already mentioned above, chances are that *it has actually been a success* at the time (otherwise why would a producer risk his money?). Classics are so most of the times because of the *theme* and the *conflict*. In this case, it is the same as with theater or literature. The films that become classics, besides being well told, are *timeless*. That is, their themes and their conflicts are present every time and in all places of Humanity. So, the first thing we must do is find the *themes* of the film and analyze how the *conflicts* were carried out.

The second most important work that a scriptwriter must do is analyze the *viewer* of the time in which the film was made. He will certainly be different from the current one. That spectator was interested in different things, which had to do with the social environment in which he was immersed. Today's viewer lives in another world -even though perhaps we are talking about thirty or forty years later- and so he is interested in different things. If we consider these two factors: theme and conflict of the previous film + current viewer, we can adapt a film and achieve an artistically innovative product, applying all the ultramodern tools we have today. These tools will be used when the director takes the script, of course, but it would be advisable that the screenwriter is aware of them, so you are not surprised when the director takes your idea towards unexpected visual effects. If you, as the scriptwriter, know the tools, you can suggest them from the script and avoid future misunderstandings.

Each film that lends itself to a remake should be analyzed as unique, but the bases, generally, are those that were mentioned above. At least, now you'll have a starting point that will not lead directly to failure. And later in the book, we will dive into the tools that will grip the interest of the viewer from the opening credits to the sequence of final ones.

A good example of a remake is *'Nine Queens'*, written by Fabián Bielinsky, in 2000 and re-adapted by Gregory Jacobs, in 2004, under the name of *'Criminal'*. Both the characters and the conflicts and themes remain the same. But the scenarios and some situations were modified; and also, in the case of the American version, they were forced to modify some issues from the original version relating to political and social conflicts that afflicted Buenos Aires at a certain moment, but that would be completely unlikely on the other side of the globe. For example, that a man wants to cash a check and that just that day there is a bank strike sounds too farfetched in the United States, but it is common currency in Argentina. So, the screenwriter chose to solve the situation in a different way, without having to stop respecting the original idea he was paying tribute to. The story was perfectly understood and turned out to be a good adaptation because the viewer to whom the film was directed had been taken into account.

The Characters

When you come up with an idea, it usually does not have so much to do with the characters, but with a *certain situation*. And while that situation requires the help of the characters to be carried forward, we take a quick look at who they are, how many we need, ages and gender, and so on, but we do not give them the importance that those issues really require. And usually we begin to develop the situation, which derives in others and forces us to add characters and new conflicts, and as soon we realize it, our head is a mess.

Just as we established some bases to orient our idea in an orderly way, we will now work more closely with the characters, so that these secrets become useful also when giving greater weight to our story.

11. Define your characters and their interrelationships

If we stop to analyze some essential characteristics of our characters, they will help us to *shape* our conflict. This is little known, since one usually does the opposite: we *adapt the characters to the conflict*. And it is not surprising, because not all conflicts can be carried forward by the same characters. For example, if we have a car accident, we will not think of a 6-year-old or a 108-year-old, right? Although... wait a moment... that is interesting!! Do you realize now, dear screenwriter? Our characters often give our idea an exciting turn, precisely because if we think about what we would *not think*, we will soon be discovering a new world of possibilities. Strong characters *make conflicts appear as if by magic*; unlike some conflicts that, because they seem strong, end up *forcing the characters*.

The first questions that we must think about are the ages, gender, social status, and so on; not to *set them in stone*, but to suggest *all possible ones* and to open the game, instead of thinking that the first one we think of is the best. Each of these details will give us other characteristics of the characters. That is, a 30-year-old, low-class man will not talk like a 15-

year-old high-class girl; nor dress the same, nor walk the same, nor react the same to the same situation. At the time of the basic idea, these characteristics are the most malleable, or *should be*. Because, in the beginning, the most important thing is not to *freeze* a certain character but to *create* it as convenient to *you* as possible. This is the time for you to ask *all* the questions that are necessary. It will do us no good to force a character to fit into a particular scene, just because it seems interesting or because we believe that the conflict is strong, and that character is plausible. Because that's another important question: *credible characters are not always interesting characters*. That is, if we have a car accident and inside the vehicle, we see a drunk 22-year-old boy (what a cliché!), it will be the most plausible of all, but will not arouse interest in the viewer in itself. We will have to continue working on the scene to put questions in the mind of the one who is watching. If, on the other hand, a 6-year-old gets out of the car, the viewer will immediately ask questions: How did that child get there? Where is his mother? How can he reach the pedals and still manage to look through the window to see where he is headed? Of course, these questions will first arise in the writer's mind, so that they can be taken to the movies; but the moment our brain bursts with questions, we will realize that this is an interesting character. And the fact that it is plausible depends on the universe we *build*.

If from the beginning we stick to the idea that the character who gets off the car *must* be a drunk, 22-year-old male, etc., just because we want to show *the irresponsibility of young people in modern societies*, we will be working on a *very* interesting theme, from a *very* boring perspective. If, instead, we say: 'I want to work on that theme; what kind of character will serve *me*?' And we make a list of the strengths and weaknesses of each possible character that we come up with to tell the story, we will be creating not only interesting characters, but a wide range of interesting *conflicts*. Think of all the conflicts derived from a scene in which a car smashes into a tree, and from which a stunned 6-year-old gets off. And also think about the relation that can be established between a conflict like this and the theme you wanted to work with in the first place. See it? Suddenly you have an interesting story in front of you, with a strong background theme, and you have a lot of possibilities to *tell* the story in an extraordinary way. That, in most cases, will leave spectators happy.

Now, very well. We have the first strong character in our story. In fact, this is one of many possible, which serves as an example here because it was interesting. It could also be a girl, or an old man, or a dog perhaps. The possibilities are endless. Let us suppose that the child convinces us because he made us ask ourselves lots of questions (which we need to write down soon, we will see why). We have to consider the characters who are going to surround him. We have the antagonist, of course, who can be his mother. Then, we have the secondary character/s, his friends, maybe. A girl may also appear to inspire him as an object of desire. In short... from our main character (in this case it's one) many others will stem. It is important that all of them are *strong* and that each one presents at least *one clear conflict* that, as far as possible, relates to the protagonist; by antagonism, by affinity, by desire, etc. In this way we will be ensuring that everyone is fixed in the *wide network of interrelations* that is generated in a film.

Now... why is it important to write down all the questions that arise in our brain? The answer is simple, but dangerous: *The viewer will ask himself the same questions when he receives the information for the first time.* If we as scriptwriters cannot answer these questions, the viewer won't either, and the film will become immediately implausible. This does not mean that he *has to* know everything. But everything he asks himself *needs to have* some answer, even if you decide not to let him know it; and if you choose that, you must also know why you do it. Know that whatever you decide to leave open due to the simple fact that you do not know how to close it, the viewer will notice. All the questions that you leave open because you don't know how to end, the viewer will notice. The more effort you put into answering your questions, the better the story will come out; and for this it is essential that you first write them down.

Examples of good movies thanks to interesting characters and strong interrelationships:

- *'Burn after reading'*, by Ethan and Joel Cohen, from 2008.
- *'When Harry met Sally'*, written by Nora Ephron, from 1989.
- *'Love actually'*, by Richard Curtis, from 2003.
- *'American Beauty'*, written by Alan Ball, from 1999.

12. Zodiac signs and Chinese horoscope

No, no... you are not mistaken. There is no printing error or confusion. You'll see why.

The zodiac signs and the Chinese horoscope, whether true or not, or whether you believe in them or not, are extremely interesting when it comes to creating characters. Let me make a small clarification here: I'm not talking about those daily horoscopes that tell you how your day will be according to the conjunction of the planets; I'm talking about unique *characteristics* that a person presents by being born on a certain date. That is, issues that involve character, personality, motivations, desires, and so on. Just by taking a zodiac sign and reading its qualities, we will find very interesting characters. And do not be surprised if you discover that a close relative meets most of those characteristics and turns out to be that sign.

What we are trying to say here is that, over thousands of years, astrologers have devoted themselves to studying human nature, finding relationships between themselves and the stars. You don't have to be a believer in the esoteric arts to put the little secret that is being revealed here into practice. You are not reading this book to invoke mysteries, but to get answers; so, it is suggested that, as a screenwriter, you should befriend these horoscopes. Read them and you will discover that there are characteristics that could suit your characters very well. And they will serve as a shield when your aunt comes and tell you that she is offended because one of the evil characters in your latest film is very much like her. After reading these horoscopes, with naturalness and eloquence, you can say, '*It is not my fault that the sign of Aries is so present in you*'.

Let's see an example from the webpage:
https://www.astrology-zodiac-signs.com/zodiac-signs/sagittarius/

Strengths: Generous, idealistic, great sense of humor
Weaknesses: Promises more than can deliver, very impatient, will say anything no matter how undiplomatic
Sagittarius likes: Freedom, travel, philosophy, being outdoors

Sagittarius dislikes: Clingy people, being constrained, off-the-wall theories, details

Curious and energetic, Sagittarius is one of the biggest travelers among all zodiac signs. Their open mind and philosophical view motivates them to wander around the world in search of the meaning of life.

Sagittarius is extrovert, optimistic and enthusiastic, and likes changes. Sagittarius-born are able to transform their thoughts into concrete actions and they will do anything to achieve their goals.

Like the other fire signs, Sagittarius needs to be constantly in touch with the world to experience as much as possible. The ruling planet of Sagittarius is Jupiter, the largest planet of the zodiac. Their enthusiasm has no bounds, and therefore people born under the Sagittarius sign possess a great sense of humor and an intense curiosity.

Freedom is their greatest treasure, because only then they can freely travel and explore different cultures and philosophies. Because of their honesty, Sagittarius-born are often impatient and tactless when they need to say or do something, so it's important to learn to express themselves in a tolerant and socially acceptable way.

The potential that zodiac signs have when thinking about the characteristics of our characters is quite clear, right? Just reading that example hundreds of questions are already triggered and our creativity is eager to get going, because when we see a character so clearly, it immediately occurs to us how the antagonist could be, who his or her partner can be, what his object of desire can be, what his objectives, what types of conflicts will confront him and so on. Interesting, right?

13. Fall in love with ALL your characters

Another issue that we should always keep in mind when developing characters is that all of them *must* generate interest. And note here that reference is not only made to the main characters; *all of them* must awaken a series of questions in us, which will be related thereafter with their conflicts and objectives. Even the most elemental character (who has dramatic importance above an extra, of course) must be there to tell us something, to oppose to something, to make us feel a certain emotion. And, although it seems like a simple detail, if we make all the characters interesting, they will leave a mark in the memory of the viewer and serve as wildcards when facing the small successive conflicts that occur in a film.

For practical purposes, the main characters will be used here as an example. It is very important that you, Mr. or Mrs. Scriptwriter, know that *there will always be* one character that you like more than the other. Sometimes it is the good one; others, the bad one. The truth is that the scale hardly ever remains balanced. Perhaps throughout the film, you feel more empathy for one first and then you switch to the opposite side. This is what usually happens. But our dear spectator is more perceptive than we would like, and in most cases notices those changes of preference. I'm not saying that the viewer or you should not *identify* with one character more than another; in fact, it is vitally important that you do so. But that does not mean that the other characters become *less interesting*. If, as writers, we give strong motivations to the protagonist, but our antagonist is weak, it will not be plausible that the protagonist has so much trouble reaching his objective, nor will it be interesting that the bad one is bad just because; that will be a cliché that will bore the viewer. And the saddest thing of all is that you will get bored too, and writing will become a turtle race. That's why you must *fall in love with all* your characters. We stopped at the main ones because they are the ones that generally make the scales tip because they are the ones that oppose each other; but you must know that the same thing happens with all of them. The stronger *all* the characters are, the better the conflicts and the more easily the story will flow.

We are going to look at some examples, in which the scriptwriter has skillfully managed to build empathetic characters and, although their motivations and characteristics may prevent one from ever identifying with them, one can understand not only their characteristics, but also their motivations. They are complicated and intricate characters, and it is often difficult to show them openly because that means that you have to delve into human evil, or physical illness or madness; and that may not always be pleasant.

- *'Dogville'*, by Lars von Trier, from 2003.
- *'Mystic River'*, written by Brian Helgeland, from 2003.
- *'The secret in their eyes'*, written by Juan José Campanella, based on the novel by Eduardo Sacheri, from 2009.

14. Awareness of desire vs. Desire of awareness

When we choose our characters, and we think about their goals and conflicts, two possibilities arise:

a. *That the character knows what he wants and starts his odyssey to get it:*
- *'Die Hard'*, written by Jeb Stuart, based on the novel by Roderick Thorp, from 1988.
- Again, *'The lord of the rings'*.

b. *That the character does not know what they want, and the odyssey consists in finding it:*
- *'The Devil Wears Prada'*, written by Aline Brosh McKenna, based on the novel by Lauren Weisberger, from 2006.
- *'The Rear Window'*, written by John Michael Hayes, from 1954.

Characters with different characteristics will derive from these two possibilities. In case 'a', our protagonist will show more security than in case 'b', and it will be more difficult to divert him from his course. Our protagonist 'b' will be dubious, will be easier to manipulate and will probably make more mistakes in his decisions. Both characters are just as interesting, and we have to define beforehand whether he knows his goal or not. In fact, this same situation can arise in all the characters of our story. What is most commonly seen in movies is that the character does not have a strong goal at the beginning, but *something happens* that sets him in motion. But the fact that he *does not know* what he has to do or where he is going is as interesting as when he does know. And this is something we often overlook because we think that a character who does not know what he wants will become a *weak* character. Well, it's not like that at all. Any character, whether he has a clear objective in life or not, can be just as boring or interesting. This is the ideal time for you as a screenwriter to get that idea out of your mind and start working on different characters. Because someone who does not know what he wants can be full of questions, he may have an *interest* in having a goal. You can wander around looking for new experiences and you can meet many interesting characters, each with a clear goal in life, to show you the possibilities of choice that you want. Notice how a small detail like this offers you hundreds of new possibilities for creating characters. Do not be afraid to dive into the human characteristics that generally cause embarrassment. Analyze them and you will not only discover new and interesting characters, but also get the viewer to identify with your character in a much more effective way since, unlike what is commonly believed, it is easier to identify with an insecure character than with one who knows what he wants perfectly, for the simple fact that we all have insecurities that no one likes to show openly. If each spectator, in the darkness of the movie theatre, can see that there is someone as insecure as he is that manages to get ahead and lead an interesting life, maybe he can do it too.

In the examples that were mentioned at the beginning of this point, we can observe that, in the case of those who know what they want, we have a policeman who learns that not only is his wife in life-threatening danger, but also an entire city; and throughout the entire movie, he maintains his goal of saving everyone. The villain of the film also has very clear objectives; so much so that only death diverts him from them.

And in the following example, we find a hobbit that needs to destroy a ring in order to save everyone from future temptations.

On the other hand, in the case of those who do not know what they want, we find in the first example a girl who goes to work in a place where she knows perfectly well that she does not want and that she dislikes, but that she thinks she is going to serve for her future, and thanks to this, she stumbles throughout much of the film, puts her main relationships at risk and ends up questioning her own existence.

And in the second case, we have a man, momentarily paralyzed by an accident, who ends up finding a goal within the film more out of boredom than out of existential necessity.

The four examples were successful at the time of release, and you will see that the fact that a character is interesting does not depend on the clarity of his objectives.

A good example of a film in which the characters go from point 'a' to 'b' and vice versa throughout the story is *'The Curse of the Jade Scorpion'*, by Woody Allen, from 2001. Once again, it would not be a bad idea to suggest that you see this man's whole filmography. But in this case, in particular, we find ourselves with people who have clear objectives, but who, by means of hypnosis, suddenly find themselves on paths completely opposite to their characteristics and motivations, which make them begin to doubt their own lives. Another way to show that just thinking about the characters' goals can build the whole story.

What are you waiting for? Get to work!

No! Wait! Do the following: take note of all the fantastic ideas that have just occurred to you and continue moving forward with the reading. Leave your notebook nearby... you will still need it.

15. What are the objectives?

Of course, this question will be asked in case our character is from group 'a' in the previous point. That is, a character who knows what he wants, so the film will deal with the adventures that he will embark on to get it. In case 'b', on the other hand, the objective will be to *find an objective*. This is clarified so that it is not mistakenly believed that point 'b' has no objective; because it does, and a very clear one at that.

As it has also been mentioned above, conflict is generally seen as the first turning point in the story. That is... the film begins with a character that wanders through life and *something* happens that makes him change his course. This is where the conflict of the film is presented, which usually *opposes* the lifestyle that our character showed at the beginning. He must arm his bag, double turn the lock of his house, and set out to fulfil his goal. Of course, this doesn't need to be so literal, it may be allegorical; but at a certain point in the film, say between the initial 5 and 15 minutes, this turning point occurs in which the central conflict manifests. It goes without saying that this conflict *must be strong enough to last the length of a movie.* That's something we all know. What we *do not generally know* is how to do it.

And again, these lines will be responsible for turning your headache into inspiration. Let's see...

It has already been mentioned that a character that is met with a situation that he would probably never face in real life, unleashes a series of questions that set the central conflict of the film in motion. And that gives rise to the revelation of the *central objective*. After that, there is a certain order for the manner in which the conflicts and objectives are presented.

So, once we have the original idea that emerged in our brain, the central conflict is created by a strong and interesting character, *not the other way around.* Then, a strong conflict leads us directly to think about the character's objective, which should have to do with the theme that we want to work on. Let's see how this is shown in an example. Let's go back to our 6-year-old who gets out of the car that hit a tree. We already have our strong character. From there -because we want to talk about the irresponsibility of young postmodern people-, conflicts arise: the child must justify to his parents the mess in which he has gotten himself, so he doesn't receive a punishment for life; that is what the child thinks. But we also have a strong conflict that is related to the central theme. The child was able to sneak into his parents' car because they work 24/7 and do not pay any attention to him. Unconsciously, he has hijacked the car to get his parents' attention. And now, instead of drawing their attention, he will see them even less because he will not be able to leave his room in years. In this situation, it is not difficult to guess what the child's objective is, nor will it be difficult to think about the vicissitudes that will divert him from it. You see? Because we placed a common character in an extraordinary situation, we got a central conflict as if by magic, a strong goal and more or less the way the story is going to develop.

As with the central conflict, if we *freeze an objective* before knowing who our characters will be, we will end up *forcing* them to fit. Following this order, however, you will soon find yourself seated in front of your computer, frantically pressing one key after another, and earnestly hoping that your fingers will follow the accelerated rhythm of your cheerful inspiration.

16. Given circumstances

This is a very important issue that we should keep in mind when developing characters, but we rarely give it the time it requires. And this is because the given circumstances, *are usually not seen in the film, but only known by the screenwriter*. It is also worth mentioning here that this is one of the issues that drives actors crazy when they read scripts, because in general, these given circumstances are not written anywhere. Most of the times, the actors must *deduct* them from the actions that are present in the script. That's ok for a spectator, *not for an actor*. The actor is the one who has to face the audience directly and tell them what happens to him in the most difficult way possible: *through actions*!! That is why you, Mr. Screenwriter, should be the first to know the given circumstances of your characters.

Now, what are the given circumstances? They are the life experiences that all your characters - *yes, yes... all of them* - lived *before* the current situation in which they are when the story begins. Each character has a past (except newborns, of course, but we recommend that you do not start a movie with the birth of a character and continue with the story in a linear way, if you do not want a full room of viewers to fall asleep), which will be reflected in his actions and in his dialogues. Some authors place point number 10 of this book within the given circumstances. Here, I decided to separate the age, social status, gender, and so on from the given circumstances because I consider that those first points must be known before the central conflict and objectives of the film are invented, whereas these experiences can be considered later. But that doesn't mean we can overlook them, as is often the case. As writers, we must know *everything* about our characters. They are our creation and it is our responsibility to do it in the most complete way possible. So, to help actors and to create strong and interesting characters, we must *invent them a past*. What school did they attend? Were they good students? Were they beaten by the band of evildoers or were they members of that band? What about their free time? Do they practice any sport? Do they read? Do they like science? In short... a million questions that help to form different types of characters. You'll confirm it when you ask yourself those questions.

The given circumstances almost never appear in the film, but they are the ones that *shape* your characters and lead them to act in one way or another at an unconscious level. As Oscar Wilde put it, '*Adulthood is the time we live trying to overcome childhood.*'

Our given circumstances mark us all as human and it would be good that the same happened to your characters.

17. The body is a consequence of the state of mind

In acting class number one, after the shy actor has introduced himself in front of all his classmates, the professor makes this statement: '*The body is a consequence of the state of mind.*' The actor raises his eyebrows and stares anxiously, waiting for the professor to speak again to explain what that means. But he doesn't; he has decided that this phrase deserves a few moments of meditation. And so it is, gentlemen; that's the truth. The actor must be aware that his body is a *tool*, because as the film is *action through the image*, he must use whatever he does with it to express what he feels. But to think about the actor is to go much further than the moment when you are sitting in front of your computer trying to explain what a character feels, and as he doesn't find the appropriate words, puff! Dialogue. You must know that the actor is not the only one who should take a few minutes to meditate on the phrase in question. And also, once you incorporate this tool into writing, you can save yourself many lines of explanatory dialogue, and incidentally you will be giving the actor a huge hand. That is why it is suggested that whenever you are presented with a situation in which you should explain how a character feels, you should use the *body movements and postures* (adding the detail of the clothing is also useful). If we have a character who is sitting in a chair, with his back hunched over, his gaze fixed on the ground a few inches from his feet, his face barely tilted and his arms loose to the sides, what impression does that give us? What is that character feeling? The answer may not be an exact one, but surely there will be two or three options, no more, and that, furthermore, through the rest of the description, it may be limited to only one. And you will have found a much more effective way than a line of dialogue to express the image you want. The actor will thank you too, because you will be relying on him to be able to tell your story.

This resource has *another* benefit. When the director takes your script to turn it into a movie, and he is confronted with this description, he will have no doubt about how to express the sadness of that character. If, instead, you simply write '*the character is sad*', you will surely end up disappointed, because the director will not be able to express what you had in mind correctly; and rightly so. Save yourself the dissatisfaction by striving a little more in that little moment where the ephemeral of thought is forever engraved on paper.

To exemplify this, a single film is suggested that will suffice to keep you entertained for a long period, seeing the thousands of different ways in which actions and feelings can be expressed throughout the body. It's the following one:

- 'Cast Away', written by William Broyles Jr., from the year 2000. In this film, we find almost ¾ parts with only one man, stranded on an island, forced to subsist on his own. You will see that it is perfectly possible to base a whole film on bodily expressions, and not only that, but also that it is vitally important that you establish all these details in your script from the first page.

18. They must undergo a transformation throughout the story

If we present a character, who is initially *insecure*, and as the film progresses, he faces different obstacles, *always with his insecurity*, and reaches the end and gets what he wants, and remains insecure, you will have made a mistake, dear Screenwriter. The characters that do not evolve throughout the film are only interesting when working on existentialism -which does not mean that existential characters are insecure, or boring, on the contrary. But, before you can risk working on these characters, you must study this range of human thought *in depth*. The rest of the characters must undergo a transformation throughout the film, due to the simple fact that, otherwise, you will be facing an epidemic of drowsiness again.

When you finish writing a script you should always study each character separately to see what he was like at the beginning and how he evolved towards the end. The problem is that if you discover that one -or worse, several- of them do not show any kind of evolution, you will have realized too late, and will have to modify much of your story. But do not worry, that's why you're reading this book: so you can prevent rather than have to mend.

To get all our characters to evolve, the first thing we must know is *how they are at the beginning of the story*. This data will become more accessible as long as you have taken into account the previous points of this book. As we establish *the main characteristics and the given circumstances* of our characters, we will delve deeper into their ways of being, their ways of speaking, of moving, of acting in general. And if we know all this about our characters, we can also know what they *are not*. That is to say, if we have a sad character, logically he will not be a cheerful character. This, which at first seems like an extreme obviousness, can be a great help to see how our characters are going to evolve later. The idea is that if you are sad at first, you can be happy at the end, etc. *Discard* and *opposition* is very useful when thinking about evolution. In this way we can know where they are headed from the beginning without having to review an entire text.

Now... It is quite easy to get the main character to evolve, because when facing different obstacles, he himself will undergo involuntary transformations. But the most common problem that is found in films has to do not with the protagonist, but with the *antagonist*. Let's see why.

Usually, the antagonist arises in the mind of the screenwriter to oppose directly to the main character. And in many cases, they believe that the problem ends there. But no. Just stand for a moment on the side of the viewer. Are you not tired of seeing bad characters that are bad from the beginning to the end and when the film ends, they have not even changed their hairstyle? This situation b-o-r-e-s! Movies usually work, although this detail makes noise in the viewer's perception, which is why few writers have the consideration that it usually deserves. The idea is not that the bad character turns good towards the end, of course. There are other ways to evolve. He may realize that he is wrong, but too late to change it; he can understand that his way of acting was not the best, even if he notices this when he is already handcuffed. In short, what we mean here is that evolution can take place even if the character does not act accordingly. And it can be *shown* -because things are *shown* in cinema- in a change of attitude, or in his way of moving, even more subtly in his way of acting. Do you understand now, dear screenwriter, why it is so important to also take into account the corporal tools?

If you think about the evolution of the main characters, you will have no problem translating it to the other characters as well. And as a result, you will get not only a movie that *works*, but a *creative* film, where even the most minor character has a purpose and undergoes changes in his way of being, as the story progresses towards the end.

Examples of interesting evolutions in the characters can be seen in the following films:

- '*Dracula*', written by James V. Hart, based on the novel by Bram Stoker, from 1992.
- '*X-Men 2*', written by Zak Penn and David Hayter, from 2003.
- '*Spider-Man 2*', written by Alvin Sargent, from 2004.
- '*Edward Scissorhands*', written by Caroline Thompson, from 1990.

The dialogues

Little insolent headaches. That's what they are. Yes, sir. When we work in movies, as mentioned above, things are *shown*. It is very difficult to work in this way due to the simple fact that, unless he listens to dialogue in a film, the spectator of classical cinema gets *bored*. Habit has won him over and he has become lazy. He, as a common spectator, does not want to have to think and relate what he sees to enter the movie's code. He prefers *to be told* what happens. So, we, as screenwriters, have to find a *balance* between what is *shown* and what is *said*, so that we can use the characteristic resources of cinema without our viewer falling asleep in the attempt.

Coming up next, secrets will be revealed to make this arduous task easier. But before, a small clarification. Since the viewer *does not mind* the dialogue, it always seems that saying something instead of showing it is a good alternative; so, it doesn't feel that writing dialogues is an *arduous* task. But, then, we find that we have failed without knowing why. But once again, you will be shown some alternatives here, not to blur the dialogue of your film, but to make each line unique and perfect.

19. Writing dialogues is like playing chess against oneself

This statement is also useful for checkers, backgammon, and other games that present a *strategy* to win. It was simply interesting to mention this sport because many people practice it in a solitary way. It is not intended to become a habit for you, but it would be good to at least try it once.

When we write the dialogue of, let's say, two characters, which is the minimum, what was mentioned above usually occurs: The writer sympathizes more with one of his characters than with the other, and this causes a *unilateral phrasing*. That is: only one of his characters speaks provocatively and ingeniously, while the other one just bore. And, in fact, the reason they should be talking is because they want to discuss what happens to *both of them*. If either of them talks nonstop explaining things, there are better resources in cinema. If one of them poses a problem and the other simply agrees with it, it bores. The interesting thing about the dialogue is that you can show several points of view *at the same time*. If we show with actions what a character thinks and then we show what his antagonist thinks, we will need at least two scenes. Only the dialogue allows access to the minds of the two characters at the same time.

For a conversation to be interesting and not only pragmatic, it is extremely effective to play chess against oneself. Basically, because this act becomes very visual. The writer must go around the table every time he changes color or turn the board. And what you will see in each case will be the *opposite* of the previous movement. When you are sitting on the side of whites, you organize your strategy to threaten the blacks, and vice versa. The problem is that every time you sit on the other side, *you already know the strategy of the other color*. This is *exactly* what happens with dialogue writing. You, as a screenwriter, know all your characters (you're supposed to have learned how to do it by now). Therefore, each time one of them speaks, you should put yourself *in his skin*. Feel what he feels, think what he thinks, and organize strategies based on *his* possibilities. And as you will know the strategies of both, you will have to contrive to have your characters talk credibly, so they don't become boring. How do you do that?

Well, for each of your characters to show only what is necessary to understand their actions, and do not become obvious or boring, you will have to think of the opposite character as the opposite in chess. When you play white, the objective is clear: to checkmate the black king, removing the protective chips (the obstacles to overcome). When you play black, the goal is also clear: checkmate the white king, etc. Each character aims at his clear goal with each move. It doesn't matter if the nearest target is to get rid of the horse you are threatening. You will always know that the final mission will be the opposite king. And just as that is breathed in every move, you must feel it in every line of dialogue. And for both characters to speak interestingly, they must be *very clear about their purpose*. Each time you put words in the mouth of a character, you have to be *on his side*. You have to *share* his wishes, his motivations and his goals. And when you change to the other character, you have to share the same with him. Only then, you will play with them *without disadvantages*.

That is why it is insisted on the fact that each character must have a *clear objective different from that of others*. If you have two characters who share the same point of view, the ideal thing is to *fuse* them into one and build a new one with a different point of view. That way, you will always have dual dialogues, always interesting dialogues.

To better anchor the above explained, the following films are recommended:

- '*Closer*', written by Patrick Marber, from 2004. Interestingly, this film was first a play, which is not surprising, considering that it was mentioned at the beginning of this book when it came to theater and its prevailing need for dialogues.
- '*The Silence of the Lambs*', written by Ted Tally, based on the novel by Thomas Harris, 1991.
- '*Wild Horses*', written by Aída Bortnik and Marcelo Piñeyro, from 1995.

20. How do the characters speak?

As we have seen above, each character must have unique characteristics, which differentiate him from the rest. Among them is *the way they talk*. Of course, this feature will be shared between characters of the same age, the same sex and the same social status. However, this is not bad; on the contrary, it helps to create realistic characters. But *it will not be realistic* that the granddaughter speaks in the same way as her grandfather, or that a woman of upper class speaks in the same way as a lower class one. Anyway, the concept is clear and easy to understand, but often more difficult to apply than it is believed. It is recommended that, when you are working on this stage with your characters, you should talk to people who meet their characteristics. It is even suggested that you give them the material to read. They will always be the first to realize if any line is failing, because they will not identify with it. And they will recommend which words to use.

Examples of different ways of speaking can be seen in:

- '*Inside Bed*' by Jorge Gaggero, from 2004. A relationship between a woman of upper class and a woman of lower class. A good place to consider this point.
- '*The Hours*', written by David Hare, based on the novel by Michael Cunningham, from 2002. In this case, the fact that one can *listen to* how a character speaks, turns out to be a film resource that the novel cannot use, and that the scriptwriter knew how to use very well when adapting. And the different linguistic codes of three different eras of the same century were treated very skillfully.

On the other hand, when writing dialogues, a new problem arises: not any line of dialogue looks good in a script. It may sound very nice when we read it *to ourselves*, but the moment the actor says it aloud, it may sound bad. That's why it's always best to write *several ways of saying the same thing*, to see which one sounds best out loud. What sounds poetic in our minds may make a noise in the spectator´s ear. If we find words that fit well with both characteristics –how a person talks in real life + how it sounds better out loud- our characters will be able to express themselves in the best way possible. Remember that *what* is said is not only important, but also *how* it is said.

21. Explanation in dialogues is boring

In general, explanations in the dialogues are used because we do not know how to express them in another way. We go crazy trying to figure out how to transmit the information to the spectator, and we begin to get so entangled, that in the end we believe that the viewer will not understand anything. So, we quickly get the problem out of our hands resorting to the safest resource of all: dialogue. The viewer speaks the same language, right? So, if I explain what happens through the characters' mouths, he will understand for sure. And yes, dear screenwriter, you will not be wrong. The viewer will understand everything, but he will also fall asleep.

As we have seen, cinema presents resources that are *unique* and too *interesting* to be wasted by a desperate screenwriter. However, it is also true that there are times when something should be said instead of shown, because of low-budget issues. Let's say that if a character survives an air crash, it will be more convenient for producers to tell it rather than show it. Needless to say, of course, to show it would be much more interesting for the viewer, since *out of sight means out of mind.* But if you don't have the budget, you need to do this, it will be much more convenient to tell it. The spectator doesn't want to see lousy visual effects either. Once again, we will have to find a balance between what is shown and what is said. And, believe it or not, you don't need to possess an extraordinary talent to accomplish this. The first thing we have to do is to *eliminate from our mind* the option of explaining a situation through dialogue. We have already seen that in some cases it is convenient, but, since it's the option that requires less work, we will leave it aside. We said that one of the resources that serves to explain through the image is *the use of the body as a consequence of the mood.* In that case, the resource serves to show feelings and often thoughts of the characters. But those are not the only things we have to tell in our story. We have to show what the character's plan is, how he intends to carry it out, where, why, when, etc., etc., etc.! At first, it seems that the only way to achieve this is through dialogue. But, once again, I'll show you how the image can prevail over the dialogue. Let's look at an example.

How about if we go back to our 6-year-old boy who just crashed Daddy's car into a tree? Don't worry, we'll pay him for the extra hours later. In that movie, we are going to have moments of action, such as the crash, the following moment, when the child gets off the car stunned by the blow, perhaps bleeding, people crowding to see the accident, and so on. But we will also have the explanatory moments, in which we will have to answer the viewer's questions:

What is that kid doing there? Why was he driving? Where is his mother? And a few more questions that you, as a good student, already noted when you came up with the idea, right? Ok. To answer these questions - without using the dialogue between the child and the police- using film resources we have to *think in images*. That is, we have to *show* the different actions that answer those questions. And the most interesting way to do this is to *break the timeline*.

That is, using *flashbacks* and *flashforwards*. We will delve into these two resources in the section 'Wildcards'. For now, the most important thing to know is that we can *take advantage of our viewer's ignorance* and reveal the information *in bits and pieces*. That is why we are talking about breaking the timeline. If instead of having the child intercepted by the police and forced to give explanations, we make him escape by rolling down a ravine, we will leave the viewer's questions in suspense and we will be able to reveal them little by little, with different images. What images? The child's parents working all day; the boy riding his rickety bicycle, looking sideways at the car; the child sitting in front of the TV, watching how a Power Ranger gets into a car and drives at full speed; the two parents leaving together in the same car, leaving the second one in the garage; etc.

In short... the possibilities, once again, are endless. All these examples are images of moments before the accident, signs that will lead to it. But we can show them when it seems more convenient; *before* or *after*. And they will work in an ever more interesting way than simply the child answering questions to the police. Explanations are always related to past or future actions. If they are *feelings* or *thoughts*, we have already seen that they can be expressed in images through the *body*. And if they are situations, we know now that they can be expressed in images through *flashbacks* and *flashforwards*.

Another problem we face when we give explanations through dialogue is *audiovisual stuttering*. Let's explain.

When a screenwriter sits down to write, he more or less imagines the film in his head (hopefully, it's more than less). What he may never know is the *weight* that the image will have when projected in the movie theater screen. But what he should know is that *undoubtedly* the image *will have more weight than he believes*. Why is it important to keep this in mind?

When a screenwriter wants to show a detail of, for example, the living room of a house, either a picture, or a book, he will put it in the description. But if that object is of the utmost importance, he will suspect that it may not be enough to just show it. He will have one of his characters comment on it. And that's where the *audiovisual stutter* arises. We will be *showing the same thing twice*. Once from the *image* and again from the *dialogue*. The *extreme close up* has a power that most writers don't know, because it's a resource that belongs to the director. Well, writer friend, it is time for you to know that this resource is, almost every time, *enough* for the viewer to pay the necessary attention to your precious object. If you make it clear in the description of the scene that this *singular-uttermost-charged-of-meaning object* must be present, the director will not fail to make an extreme close up of it and your characters will then be able to dedicate themselves to talking about more interesting things. And you can, by the way, keep the explanations for later, leaving the viewer with that object in his head without understanding why. And that will arouse interest. Remember that that is what you are always striving for: keeping the viewer *interested* in your film.

22. Eternal monologues are almost always failures

Luckily, this is one of the mistakes that are discovered fastest in a script; because we see that the script is neat and balanced, and suddenly we find the name of a character in the middle, very prolix, with darker letters, and underneath it, a page and a half of verbiage. When a character speaks so much at once, without interruptions, in most cases it is a mistake. Of course, there are exceptions, but they are the least and in general they are casual, not sought after. And it also turns out to be that, for the good fortune of the ignorant scriptwriter, there are cases in which an excellent actor can carry out a monologue in an interesting way. These actors usually have very good training in theater. But look at all the details you must have in your favor to make the scene look good: an actor with an impeccable theatrical training + an excellently written monologue + an overly talented director, who can film that moment in the most dramatic way possible, so that the viewer does not realize that he has been watching the same thing for five minutes. A monologue saves us a lot of cinematographic time and a lot of money on the set. But if the scene goes wrong, our viewer will not be happy, and he will not recommend our film. You're probably thinking that *one* bad scene does not necessarily lead to a bad movie, but if we find this error the first time in the script, it'll probably betray us a few more times. And this is because extensive monologues have to do with an inability of the screenwriter to *show* instead of *telling*. Monologues are directly related to the previous point: the explanation in the dialogues. If a character speaks so much at once, surely it will have to do with the explanation of something. His feelings, his thoughts, his plans, etc. We have already seen that there are better ways to do this.

In addition, there is another question that we must consider. For a character to speak out loud, another character must be *listening*. ALWAYS. Shakespeare's monologues are only plausible in Shakespeare's works. In all other cases, there must be another character paying attention to what the first is saying, owing to the simple fact that it will not be credible for a character to speak alone; unless he is crazy, drunk, blah, blah, blah... It just happens to be that the crazy and drunkards in cinema, as secondary characters, are generally present to validate monologues. In this book, we do not consider them viable tools because they bore spectators.

Now, returning to the person who listens, who must always be present in the scene, it will cease to be interesting -if he ever was-, the moment he ceases to be someone with a goal, personal characteristics and unique given circumstances, and becomes a *listener*. The only function of a listener is to *justify* the monologue of the one who speaks. None of your characters should be so uninteresting at any point in the script. That is why it is suggested that you leave monologues aside. You will save yourself long verbal explanations, you will not have to depend on a great actor or a better director, nor will you have to study all of Shakespeare's monologues to make your own more or less interesting. Take advantage of the tools that cinema offers and *show* what you want to tell or write theater. We have already seen that it is an option as viable as any other.

23. Start your dialogues in the middle of the action and avoid fillers

When we think of writing the dialogue between at least two characters, we tend to start with a presentation. One says, 'Hello,' then the other says 'Hello, how are you?' And by the time we get to the interesting part, the viewer has fallen asleep. The ideal thing is to begin *in media res*; that is, *in the middle of the conflict*. (We could have said the second thing directly, but the expression 'in media res' is very common in the field of writing. It is time for you to become friends with it, because you will probably become a successful screenwriter and it will look good. Use it every so often.) One of the strategies you can use to avoid boredom in the viewer is not to get rid of the beginnings of the conversations, but to *use them as tools that only you will know*. In this case, it works like the given circumstances. You can write the whole conversation, from beginning to end, and then delete from the beginning to the interesting part. Then, your characters will start the scene directly in it. The same thing happens with fillers and expressions like '*um*', '*I mean...*', '*I...*'. You can use them in the first version of the script but be sure to make them disappear by the time of the final draft. We imagine that a character may hesitate before speaking, but the actor will know perfectly how to deal with it. And if the pause is not enough, the editor can always stretch the shot of the listener a little more. Instead, the actor will feel more uncomfortable if he has to respect all the tricks you put in his dialogue, which also have no dramatic significance. Of course, they serve to define a character's way of speaking, but you have to be very careful when using them, because as mentioned above, sometimes it does not sound the same in the mind as when we hear it out loud. It is best that you always keep the dialogues as short and accurate as you can in the final draft. That will give the actor freedom to express himself as he sees fit.

The Scenarios

Scenarios are as important in a script as any of the previously mentioned points. The difference is that they are seldom given the importance they deserve. And this is because so many things have happened in so many different scenarios, that the viewer does not seem to mind that situations are carried out in the most classic or more unusual places, without explanation or dramatic importance. But that is not considered viable for this book. There is no interest in showing you how to write a common script that takes place anywhere. The intention is to show you as many resources as you need, so that tomorrow, if you do not use them, it's because you *chose not to do it* and not because you *don't know how to do it*. Scenarios are tools. And we will show you how to use them consciously.

24. The place must be another character

When the characters were mentioned above, it was said that they must all have *unique personal characteristics, given circumstances* and *an objective that does not coincide with any other*. Scenarios have these characteristics as well. That is why they can -and should- be considered as characters.

Each place has a different purpose. A restaurant, for example, has as its first purpose to *feed the diners*; it also has a second purpose which is to *bring people together*. When one character is sitting opposite another in a restaurant, he has no choice but to talk to him. That is why they are a classic of important conversations. Restaurants also have the characteristic of being *public places*. That is why they are taken into account also if what we want is to cause a scandal and for some of the characters feel uncomfortable. For this purpose, buses or crowded streets are also useful. The problem is that, in general, what screenwriters have in mind is that the scenario should, for example, be public. But to put it eloquently, *each stage has its own spirit*. Even if we think that the best thing is for the scene to take place in a restaurant, we must take into account that each restaurant is unique (excluding fast food chains). Each one has its lighting, its soundproofing, its distribution, and its decoration. And each of these details influences the scene as one character more. That is why you should *always* consider it as such.

Another classic example is the bedrooms. Those places that lend themselves to 'intimacy'. The writer often thinks that if he needs a married couple to talk about an important topic, it is best to put them in the bedroom. And then we see the characters, leaning against the back, each one reading a book and looking sideways because they know they have to talk. The tension is perceived in the air. The viewer also knows that the characters have to speak. And then... the famous audiovisual stutter arrives. The woman looks up from her book at the man and says, '*Albert... we need to talk...*'. As if it were not obvious enough for the viewer to understand what was happening, the characters comment on a situation that is already very clear through the image. And our viewer sits in the armchair, wondering when they will reach the interesting part. How ugly, right? We do not want him to think that about our beloved movie. He does not know all the vicissitudes we went through as we wrote; all the sweat and frustration that ran down our cheeks. But he does not care about that. He just wants to be told a story; and we're not doing it, apparently. So, dear screenwriter, keep in mind these little details. Each scenario is going to say something for itself. It is up to you to find out *what*, to be able to adjust it to its *how*.

We are going to mention 3 examples in which the scriptwriter has been insightful enough to think of the stage as one more place:

- '*Cube*', written by André Bijelic and Vincenzo Natali, from 1997. In this film the stage is so, so important, that everything else - characters, times, conflicts, etc.- revolves around it. The entire movie has been built as if it were the main character and not a living being. This is said for you to consider the importance that we can give it, although it is not essential to consider it.
- '*What Dreams May Come*', written by Ronald Bass, from 1998. This example is placed to show where -according to the script- a person goes when he dies. The interesting thing to take from this is that the

protagonist, while living, had a lot of contact with the artistic world of painting and thanks to that, he builds his own paradise with real paint. A lot of general shots are seen in this film because we constantly try to show the dramatic importance of the place where characters are immersed.

- '*Barton Fink*', written by Ethan and Joel Cohen, from 1991. In this case, it is a man who wants to write, but feels that his creativity has abandoned him. The place where he writes is a hotel room that does nothing but deepen that terrible anguish that lack of inspiration produces. Instead of putting the character in a bar, drinking one cup of coffee after another, his emotions are reflected in the overwhelming confinement that particular scenario promises.

25. Why THIS place and not any other?

That is the question that follows the previous point. Once we realize that the stage is another character, we have to analyze it in depth. Just as we ask ourselves 'why this character and not any other?' we must ask the same about the scenarios. Because when we first think about the characters, we definitely don't choose them randomly, we have already seen why. We should always ask ourselves what the best scenario is, but not only because we believe that there is always *one* that is the *indicated* one, but also because sometimes we think that *an action could never happen in a given scenario*, but if we take the time to verify it, we may end up finding that the scenario we thought improbable ends up being the most appropriate. We had already gone through this situation with the selection of characters, remember? That moment when we realized that a six-year-old kid crashing a car could be very interesting? Good. The same will happen with scenarios if you take enough time to analyze them all. Because maybe we could think that if a character has to tell his brother that their father has a terminal illness, we certainly will not think of a bus, for example, full of people... will we? It would be risky. A difficult situation to develop, right? But NOT impossible, and certainly as plausible as we can build it. Taking this situation forward in a place like that can be very difficult, but it will be radically more interesting. Mr. Scriptwriter, *don't shy away from complicated situations*. They're going to cost you a lot more work, but you'll feel great when you learn to master them. That is why you are encouraged to always consider as many scenarios as possible before deciding on one. It has already been seen that the *unimaginable* can be as *possible* as any other. You can even resort to the resource of *opposition* here. If you have a character that is depressed and all he wants is to be locked in his room with headphones on, listening heavy metal so loudly that it is possible for the viewer to listen as well, perhaps it is best that something happens then -it will depend on your talent to find out what- which forces the character to attend, for example, a party. Notice how small conflicts and questions immediately arise and the scene suddenly becomes interesting. The possibilities are endless, so bear them in mind.

26. Common scenarios

A brief mention will now be made of some of these common places that seem very pragmatic and comfortable, but which are most interestingly boring. There is a very nice example to show you: ladies and gentlemen, I present you... *the living room*! What's wrong with the living room? Well, if there *was* anything wrong, maybe it would be interesting. What happens with the living room of the house is that it is one of the safest places to develop a scene. Not for nothing, almost all sitcoms have a living room. It's so common, that it's critical for a format in which you work the least number of possible scenarios. All the characters pass at some point through the living room, so, we can then deduce that it is not uncommon for them to pass again, but this time stay talking. And that's true. But once again, I ask you as an artist, do you want your script to be one of a bunch or do you prefer to stand out from the rest? Then, follow these instructions and we suggest that you do *not* shy away from complicated situations, we ask that you please run in the opposite direction to common scenarios. They may serve you initially to work a little more closely on the characters' actions, what they have to say, and so on. You can place them in the living room while you delve deeper into the skin of each of your characters to work on the dialogues better. But once you are clear on this, *think about other scenarios*. All the ones you can imagine. And notice how they will influence your characters. Even if you have to resort to the most unusual, the most unlikely, you might think it is always better to have options to discard and not have to choose between a few boring ones.

Other classics mentioned above are bars and restaurants. The same. Safe places if ever there were ones... For the cinema, a bar is like a stage for the theater, that is, a place where actors appear and chat. It won't look bad, you can be sure of that. But you are going to waste the opportunity to make your story even more fascinating, and believe me, that it is not so difficult, which makes it even more of a shame for them to be wasted.

Want more examples? The bedroom, squares and parks, the kitchen, the sidewalk, the interior of a car... Hasn't it ever occurred to you to think why these scenarios always appear in films? They are safe places. As safe as the annoying voiceover, but we'll talk about that later.

Think, search, analyze, ask, walk, take photos, investigate; in the daytime, at nighttime, under the rain or the sun, in the cold... Trust that the right place is right in front of your eyes. Do not waste it due to lack of time or comfort.

27. Visit the scenarios that you have in mind. By day, by night. Each place has unique qualities. You will come up with ideas.

This is a little secret that this book gives you for having been brave enough to reach this instance. We talked about the spirit of the stages, of their unique and unrepeatable qualities; and it has also been said that the scenarios that seem impossible can be viable and interesting. Well, now that you have a list with at least 32 different scenarios to choose from for your next scene, you can start discarding some. Okay... a little more than *some*. Let's say you have 4 or 5 of the most interesting ones. With this list in mind, go out and walk the streets. Enter as many different places in the same category as you can. Let yourself be carried away by the spirit of each place and imagine your characters in there. This will help you visualize your scene more deeply. Remember that the image has a weight with which the director is more familiar than you. This way you can finish choosing the most convenient scenario. And, as you do that, you will meet places that will be useful for other scenes. You are going to have new ideas, so it is also suggested that you go out with paper and pencil.

It looks like a to-do list. And it is. If you believed that only a little talent and a typewriter were necessary to write, you will have realized by now that everything is not so easy. It is not mandatory that you leave your house to write a good script. Nothing contained here is *mandatory*. The only intention is to pass on as many secrets as possible, so that your scripts end up opening doors instead of filling drawers.

The Wildcards

In this part of the book I will mention some items that are very useful when writing scripts. Some make our work more organized; others help us to enrich the stories, and there are also those who get us out of trouble when we feel that the story is getting out of hand. Interesting, right?

But first, a warning. It has already been explained that sometimes, things that get us out of trouble are *the easiest,* but *the least interesting.* However, it is important that you know them. But keep in mind that the viewer perceives *everything.* And if you use any of these wildcards out of fear that your story gets out of hand, he will notice. And he will not like it very much. It will depend on you to find the necessary balance to know that you can risk much more than you thought, because ultimately, you will always have one of these wildcards at hand. From this humble perception, the best thing that you can do as an artist is to *risk everything.* And if these wildcards serve to bring you the necessary safety to jump into the abyss, it will have been worth the effort.

28. Characters and/or objects that seem to have nothing to do with the story

To be able to understand this, we first need to know something that, while useful, sometimes collaborates more with our laziness than with our ingenuity and makes us lose our path. This is: *in movies, we can place characters and / or casual objects that go unnoticed from beginning to end.* It seems that the same has been stated in the title of this point, but if you observe correctly, it hasn't. Because one thing is that something *has nothing to do with the story* and another very different one is that it *goes unnoticed.* That's why these wildcards seem to have nothing to do with the story, but *in reality,* they are just going unnoticed. And the best thing about this is that if we do not use them in the end, the viewer will not have noticed them.

It turns out that cinema *shows* what it wants to tell, right? A well-known fact at this point. But it is also true, and this is where we take advantage ourselves, that cinema *cannot cover everything*. There are many things about the image that are unapproachable, especially on large, open shots. When the viewer sees these images, he pays attention to the most important thing, and *discards* the rest. This dismissal is the one that plays in our favor to be able to apply our wildcard. If we place characters that look like extras and/or objects that look decorative, the viewer will not notice them. And we can show them several times throughout the film, and in the end... *they will solve the story for us*! Yes. You read correctly. If we can show these objects and/or characters in a way that is *subtle enough* to go unnoticed but *visible enough* to be registered in the mind of the viewer, when we show that that was the key to the movie, it will be justified, and the spectator won't be able to object anything. He will have to sit back and swallow the dissatisfaction of not having been able to guess the end.

The most interesting thing about this little secret is that practically anything can *be that object* and any extra can *be that character*. A trait of ours as writers is to find relationships between the most unusual things. We always find a way to establish a link between practically anything. It is part of our talent. And this is a way to use it in our favor, because you can place objects and characters without even understanding why they are there and find the relationship as the story progresses. Really interesting, right?

Now... not everything is simple, of course. Some details must be taken into account. The first thing to know is that these wildcards should *always be presented at the beginning of the film*. We cannot simply make them appear as if by magic five minutes before the end of the film, because we will be showing no respect to the viewer. However, presenting them at the beginning should not be a complication, because if we place them there and then we do not use them, they will also go unnoticed. The other thing we should consider is that the stranger the object or the character is, the better the spin we can give to the film, but -yes, yes... but again- the *riskier* it will be and the bigger the chance it will come out wrong. However, as it has been said before, these lines welcome you to risk. Precisely that is why we offer these wildcards.

29. Plot outline

The plot outline is a very effective tool to perform an orderly job. Most screenwriters use it because it allows us to have the whole movie *in the palm of our hand*. It serves to organize the scenes and the presentation of characters, it helps us to see what scenarios are going to appear in each moment, and so on. All this is achieved because, in a plot outline, *the story is organized in a single page*.

Another way to build the structure is to use file cards, placing each scene in one of them and then ordering them on the table or sticking them on the wall. The idea is to make the film *as visual as possible*. What some writers also do is separate the characters by color, so when we see the notes, we will know who appears in each scene. This helps a lot to see that we haven't shown a character in a while because we got excited and there is another one that dyes all the file cards the same color, and so on. Not that this is a bad thing. Maybe it was our intention that it be so, but it is always better to make sure, so that we receive the least amount of surprises possible. Writing scripts is magic, and no magician likes to be surprised by his audience, for that is *his* job.

The file cards also serve to organize *how we are going to tell the story*. That is, what we are going to let the viewer know first and after. We can take the notes and place them in the order that we think is most convenient. Remember that *breaking the timeline* gives our script strength.

We are going to provide an example of how a file card for our script would look like:

Theme of the scene: car crash against a tree.
Characters present: a *6-year-old* first, then *extras* and *two policemen*.
Scenario: A little traveled dark street.
<u>Beginning of the scene</u>: The child maneuvers the car uncomfortably. The car gets out of his control progressively.
<u>Middle of the scene</u>: The child crashes against a tree.
<u>End of the scene</u>: The kid rolls down a ravine and escapes.

It is very important to make a small clarification here. Perhaps it's obvious to say that *all the scenes must have a beginning, a middle and an end,* but we'll clarify it anyway. If we have a scene that does not meet this feature, we probably have a useless scene, because we'll have a scene that *is not telling anything.* All the stories begin with a presentation, a development and an ending. If you believed that this only had to be achieved in the whole film, you were mistaken. Remember when we talked about chess. Remember that to access the king, we first have to get rid of those annoying pawns that work as obstacles. The film works the same way. We must go step by step to achieve the ultimate goal. And each of these steps implies a *minor conflict to solve*; that is, *a smaller story to tell, but which is just as important.* And although this rule must be followed strictly for each sequence, it is very important that each scene has something to tell, however small. And it is just as important that no scene ends where it started, with no evolution or new information revealed. This will be a waste of time that will bore the viewer.

Now, back to the plot outline mentioned above. The example has shown a very practical way of placing the details that should appear in them. Remember to color them so they become as visual as possible. By doing it, we will be doing a favor to our ability to remember and we will leave aside the feeling that we need medication for memory.

30. The treatment

This is the step that follows the plot outline and it's the last one before the script. When we already have our organized story in the file cards and we are satisfied with it, we can begin to deepen into each one of them. Following the example above, we can add the detail of the exact scenario; we can write step by step how the scene is going to unfold; we can calculate the estimated time that it will last; we can also mention what the characters are going to talk about, etc. There are no rules for plot outlines or treatments. The ultimate purpose of them is that you can clearly visualize the story in your head. Remember that the more visual the movie becomes, the better.

The treatment is the narration of each scene in order, in script format, without the presence of dialogues. But again, if you notice that suddenly, in the midst of writing a plot outline or a treatment, you are seized by a voracious inspiration and want to write all the dialogues in that scene, do not deprive yourself of doing so. Anything that helps you develop your creativity is welcome. You will always have time to modify or discard it if you change your mind. These are *tools*, not *laws*. You can take them into account if you want to or write your script from scene one to the last one without stopping. But I tell you that if you discover flaws in your idea, it will be much less laborious to modify them from the plot outline or treatment than from a developed script.

As mentioned above, the treatment instance has the good quality of allowing us to work on separate details that will then go together, to work as if they were the only thing present in the film. For example, if we already know that in the scene described in the file card corresponding to the plot outline there is going to be a car accident, we can stop there for an instant, remove all the other issues from the middle and stop to think about that street, which is going to carry out our conflict in the best possible way. We can build a list with all that we can think of, without the fear of thinking that we may deviate from the story, or that we will lose the connection with the other facts and such. We can also think of the model of the car, which one is the most likely to be driven by a child, its color, we can also think about the weather. In short... the treatment gives us the possibility of working on the detail to the maximum, in the most orderly way possible.

31. Ellipsis

These little rascals generally have two completely different objectives that derive from the base of *hiding information*.

The first of these arises from a *practical* matter. There are times when we omit information to make the film more bearable. If we are in front of a *road movie* (one of those films that are developed almost entirely on roads) about a group of friends that goes from LA to NY, we will have to resort to the ellipsis in many occasions, unless we want to have a group of spectators sitting in the movie theater for three days. That is, the first use of ellipsis has a pragmatic purpose: organizing the timeline in such a way that it keeps an interesting rhythm, eliminating dead times and without a dramatic goal.

The second use, by far one of the most interesting resources in cinema, is the one that serves as a wildcard. In this case, we have a *conscious deprivation of information*, through a temporary ellipsis, with an *entirely dramatic purpose*. The last part is the most important of this resource. We repeat: '*with an entirely dramatic purpose*'. To ellipse a situation because it has become cumbersome and we do not know how to explain it, is not valid for this book. Dramatic ellipsis must have a different *justification* from '*I didn't know how to continue*'. There is no intention here to encourage lazy screenwriters. Much less if they are going to waste such a fascinating resource as this. Let's see.

One of the hallmarks of dramatic ellipsis is that, like a character or a strange scenario, it *triggers questions in the viewer's mind* that keep him interested in our movie. Again, it is worth noting here that these questions will first arise in the mind of the screenwriter, so it is recommended that you also write them down. When the viewer is waiting for us to show him something we suddenly conceal, he opens his mouth, raises his eyebrows, blinks a couple of times in amazement, and asks where the hell they took the most interesting part of the scene (because of course, you will choose *that* part to ellipse). This feature is very interesting because it *promises* interested viewers.

But you will have to justify your triggering if you do not want tomatoes thrown against the big screen. We are going to provide an example. Let's give a warm welcome to... our 6-year-old! Applause! Applause!

Imagine that instead of showing the crash we see that the child is bored at home alone. Then we see that he goes to the garage, gets into his parents' car, grabs the steering wheel and makes a noise as though he were driving at full speed, but everything with the engine off and without leaving home. And then... puff! Ellipsis. We show the same child away from the city, walking alone, all filthy, while listening to threatening police sirens in the distance. We have ellipsed the whole crash and also installed the bug of interest in the mind of the viewer. That will play in our favor, because he will ask himself many questions, but certainly not imagine that the child has crashed his parents' car! And from there we have a ton of information to give the viewer, which we can organize as we see fit. Remember that this is a story about the irresponsibility of postmodern youth, where parents work all day, devoting less and less time to the upbringing of their children. We also have a frightened child because he does not want to be punished, since he only tried to attract the attention of his parents, etc. Now notice how the ellipsis made our child an even more interesting character. Because we not only have to tell the viewer (in images) about his motivations and goals, but now we also have the fact that he *does not know* that the child hit a car on our side. We have a lot of material to get us working. That, plus some creative seasoning, from a talented screenwriter like yourself, will certainly give us an interesting story. Dramatic ellipses are cool, right?

32. The flashback

The flashback is a resource that is generally used to *display* information rather than *saying* it. This is why the resource is promoted as a much more effective tool than an explanatory dialogue.

When we resort to this resource, we do it to tell something that has happened in the past. And if we have something to say about a past event, it is because we did our job well and created excellent *given circumstances* for our characters; or good enough to have dramatic significance worthy of being shown.

Flashbacks also serve to maintain the tension in the viewer, because they are very practical in the explanatory moments of the film. We have already seen that action, in general, is what interests the viewer. But we cannot keep up the tension for a long time because he simply will not stand it. We must interweave actions with explanatory moments, which are also necessary so that he can understand what happens. So, in order to avoid that annoying blabbering, we can use some beautiful images from the past that we will bring up to explain feelings or thoughts or perhaps some situation that our character lived at some point and now has him, for example, worried.

The flashback allows us to get inside the characters' minds. Just as literature can tell practically everything, cinema also has its resources. And besides, nothing better than an image to revive a memory. Even if we do not have enough resources to show an air crash instead of telling it, we can use confusing, out of focus, bright and fast images that only appear during a couple of frames that are interspersed with the verbal explanation. So, as you can see, whether it's a few images or a whole scene, flashbacks are the cinematographic resource par excellence to dive into our characters' memories.

The flashback also serves to *mislead the viewer*, as we show images of the past that a character may remember but *were not actually like that*. As this resource relates to the past, the viewer is generally confident that the source is accurate, but if we stop to think for a moment, where has it been seen that someone remembers a situation exactly as it happened? Even several witnesses of the same fact will give us different versions of what happened.

(See: *'Citizen Kane'*, written by Herman J. Mankiewicz and Orson Welles, from 1941). Therefore, with the flashback we always have the *viewer's accustomed trust* in the truthfulness of facts on our side. We can use that confidence to mislead him about some fact that we do not want to show him yet and entertain him with a very plausible explanation, but one completely different from the truth of the facts. This can also help the *famous plot twist*. So, apparently, the flashback is another *proper resource of cinema* worthy of being exploited, right?

33. The flashforward

This feature is less used in film than the flashback, although it is equally useful and interesting. It is more difficult to apply because this tool shows *the future*. And as we all know, the future is always changing.

It is usually used to show the *expectations* that some character has about a certain situation that is to come. Resuming the example of our little boy, this resource would be used to show how the parents give a spectacular reprimand to the boy and lock him in his room for life, just as he gets off the crashed car and sees the police approaching. What we are showing is the *motivational thinking* that makes him set off to escape.

The flashforward is always related to virtual situations; unlike the flashback, which usually shows facts that actually took place. In this case, we do not have the viewer's trust on our side. We cannot show him something of the future and expect him to believe it blindly.

However, this resource is also preferable to the eternal verbal explanation. Just as the flashback serves to get us into the characters' *memories*, the flashforward gets us into their *thoughts*. It also help us to show specific characteristics of the different ways of being of each one. Hundreds of examples of flashforwards have already been seen in the cinema where a character imagines that he throws a chair over the head of his unbearable boss, and immediately afterwards we see that the employee smiles and nods as he listens to his boss giving orders nonstop. In this case, we are using an extremely visual tool, which shows the character's mind and makes the viewer identify with him. Think if it is not much more interesting to show that, than to organize a post-work scene where the character talks to his friends and *tells them* how much he dislikes his boss.

Another practical purpose of a flashforward is to show the plan that a character intends to carry out. If, instead of seeing him *telling* another one his vile and strategically organized plan, we *show it in actions* in a flashforward, we will be using a cinematographic resource, and incidentally we will avoid the thread of drool that usually hangs from the mouth of a sleepy spectator.

Although these two resources are well known by any scriptwriter who has read any theory book about screenwriting, here they are considered wildcards because they are faithful to the cinema and it is very difficult for them to look badly in a scene, simply because anyone would like to be able to *see* what another one imagines or remembers. The viewer will be satisfied in almost all cases, because since he cannot visually access *his own* thoughts and/ or memories, at least he can see *someone's*. Do not be afraid to use these wildcards. Even if you find it difficult at first to introduce them, they will not look badly, and you can practice safely until you become an expert, practically without any risk. Cool, uh?

34. The voice-over

At this point, you must have a slight idea of this book's opinion about the voice-over. It is not considered to be, by far, the best resource that can be used in film. Anything that collaborates with *telling* something instead of *showing* it is a waste of the great unique tools that cinema has. But, although we don't want to admit it, it should be considered as a wildcard, for the same reason as the wonderful resources of dramatic ellipses, flashbacks and flashforwards: *they always look good*. And this is also because the viewer cannot hear other people's thoughts in real life, and he likes to be able to listen to someone else's, even in fiction. We appreciate that no one can read our thoughts but pray we can read those of others. Above all, those of our partner, right?

Listening to what a character thinks fascinates the viewer, calls his interest, and makes him identify with him; it also gives the story fluency. But the voice-over is NOT a proper resource of the cinema. We have already seen it. The voice-over does not *show*, but it *tells*. And while it is easier to explain something through words, it is much more interesting that the viewer sees it. It is no coincidence that the voice-over is usually associated with some of the characters through the image (except in the cases of omniscient narrators, of course, so common in documentaries), and it also tells something that relates to what is being shown. This often causes audiovisual stutter: we see that the story becomes more bearable because we use the wildcard, and before we know it, it gets out of hand and we end up telling *the same thing* that is being shown.

It is also common to see in movies how the voice-over replaces monologues that would otherwise be unrealistic. Instead of seeing that a character is talking alone, we hear his voice-overtelling his vile and strategically organized plan or explaining why he is acting the way he is. My friend, the voice-over does not bother anyone, but considering the magnitude of your talent, a choice of this type will always be a waste.

The voice-over is a resource that is widely used in film adaptations of literary novels. We have already seen that literature delves *a lot* into the characters' thoughts and that -in that format- is sometimes enough to explain actions that are carried out, which perhaps are not even told. This drives screenwriters crazy, because they find themselves suddenly sinking in a world of pure thought and no action. And they realize that if they want the same thing to be understood in cinema, they must resort to voice-over, otherwise they will need much more time to tell the story through images, a time that the film does not offer in generous quantities. That's why we tell you that the voice-over is a resource that does not bother, but we warn you to be careful when using it, because we have already seen how comfortable and pragmatic is not always *interesting*.

35. The hateful signs that indicate temporality

This is a wildcard that has the word *laziness* written all over it. The cinema has so many visual resources to indicate temporality that seeing a sign on the screen makes us wonder how much affection the screenwriter has for his own work.

Each moment in History has some image that functions as its icon. It can be a painting, an automobile model, a wardrobe, a stage decoration, a horse drawn carriage, a music group, the characters' behavior, technological objects, environmental pollution, etc., etc., etc.! Hundreds, thousands of visual resources. Once we understand this, we realize how much we are wasting using these wildcards. Of course, they look good. Of course, no one will notice. Of course, they are insignificant details. So many things are taken for granted in cinema that we forget *how* to write cinema. If we overlook these details, it is because we are not asking ourselves if there is any better way to show things. And as we get used to this, shortly after, we will be happy with the voice-over, and when we want to remember, we will be writing literature for cinema. And there go the scripts, one after another, piled inside the drawer. A pity.

Consider these warnings an exaggeration, if you wish. But be aware that not everything that is customary in movies turns out to be the best resource. Take advantage of your creativity and do not be afraid to break with the established. In the end, if you are not convinced, you will have validated the practice for a future experience and you will be able to put, only for this time, the nice little sign to show temporality that will make you look good. The only desire of these lines is that you have alternatives. A talent like yours surely can give much more than a simple and safe habit.

36. Do not start a script thinking about the genre. Build a structure and adapt it to the genre you want later.

This wildcard helps us to start writing without any previous unnecessary complications. The first thing we need to know in order to use it is that *all genres are interchangeable*. That is, we can take a horror film and turn it into comedy, turn a melodrama into an action movie, etc. That's why if we say, *'I'm going to write a comedy'*, we'll be putting obstacles in our way that will not collaborate with our creativity. It's better if we start to write the story, and then see what genre is best suited to our idea. Afterwards, if we are infatuated with some particular genre, we can see what its characteristics are (detailed later in this book, of course) and mold it to our idea. *It is much easier to adapt a genre to an idea, than an idea to a genre.* So do not worry about this detail from the beginning. It is preferable to use that time to think about the means of exhibition, durations, characters, objectives, conflicts, questions, and so on. You will have enough to occupy your mind with just that.

37. Sit in a bar to listen to people's conversations

Wait... what? What is this about? How unethical! How am I going to sit in a bar with the sole purpose of listening to what others are talking about?!

Don't worry, this idea has a purely educational interest. You are not being asked to *make judgments* based on what you hear, but something much more interesting. What is proposed here is to learn to filter *what* is being said from *how* it is being said. Over time you will notice that the bar conversations are always similar: work, home problems without too much relevance, organization of plans, and anecdotes. What you should learn is to focus your attention on the *way* these conversations are being carried out. Each will have a different *tone*, a different *volume*, a different *goal*. You will also find differences between the conversations depending on whether they are spoken by two women, by two men, by a group of women, by a mixed group, etc. Take note of what catches your eye. And if you can, try to listen to conversations that have a similar theme, pay attention to *differences in the forms*.

Don't worry too much about morals and ethics. If you think that it is wrong to get into people's lives, dear screenwriter, you can start thinking about changing profession, because that is precisely the whole purpose of our business. And if you think this statement is invalid, ask yourself a simple question: *what is the purpose of writing, if you do not want to transmit anything to anyone?* Know now that the more you influence people's lives, the better you will feel as a writer. It's time to accept it and move on.

38. Watch all the movies that relate to your idea

Sometimes, when we come up with an idea, we often think that it has already been made, that it will not be original, or we relate it immediately to films dealing with the same thing, and we think that the viewer will criticize us for plagiarists. So, what you have to do to avoid this is to *pay homage to those movies that relate to your idea*. Let's take a look at an example.

If we use laser sabers in our film trying to be original, we will not surprise anyone. The viewer will immediately relate our movie to the *'Star Wars'* saga and will want to watch those movies instead of yours. But if, on the other hand, we *anticipate* the spectator's assured criticism and, knowing that the laser sabers are an icon of that saga, we *quote* parts of the previous films in ours, we will be telling the viewer: *'Okay. I know that I'm not original with my idea, but who wouldn't like to pay homage to a saga like that one?'* The viewer will be delighted. And he will think: *'Let's see what's new about this movie...'* and he will open up to you to show him everything you want, without even thinking about the taboo of plagiarism.

On the other hand, when you look at all the films that relate to your idea, you realize that there are many more ways to tell the same things than you believed. That will make you wonder if your way is the best way to convey what you want with your movie. And that is already a great step to trigger your creativity. *Doubt* can be a very productive friend when it comes to exercising talent: it can lead you to unexpected *certainties*. Do not be afraid to face movies that speak the same language. In no time, you will be engaged in conversation with them.

Rarely considered details

There are some issues that should always be taken into account, but since they do not have to do with theoretical material per se, they are rarely discussed. That is why, as this is a peculiar book that offers more secrets than theory, you will have the opportunity to go beyond the ordinary, to find out that there is much more to see than you ever imagined. Perhaps, later on, you can translate that expanded vision into your own talent. These lines will be satisfied, knowing that they have fulfilled their fundamental purpose.

39. The average viewer of your story

As you have already noticed, dear screenwriter, throughout this book we have developed different points; some more related to each other than others. But in *all cases* the spectator has been mentioned. He is the one who is going to sit in the movie seat waiting for a well-told story, he will be the one who builds an opinion about our work and will also be the one to recommend it in case he considers it to his liking.

The spectator has an unimaginable power over us. We are servants here and we have to meet his expectations. Why do we do it? Due to the simple fact that we want to transmit our dreams, our desires, and our ideals to him. We need him to help us go beyond our own lives. He is the elixir of our immortality. That is why he has been mentioned at every point in these lines and in every revealed secret. Now, a whole point will be dedicated to him alone.

When the *average viewer* is mentioned, the intention is to become aware of *the one we speak to directly* as screenwriters. Of course, the films are seen by many more, but there is *one* viewer that we want to tell something to face to face. And we need to know that he exists, and we *must* always keep him in mind so that our film works in the best possible way. We cannot encompass them all. Even in films that are 'for the whole family' there are preferences. It is not a question of inventing it, but of *discovering* it. Your average viewer is out there, queuing while deciding what movie to watch, and he must know that there is one for *him*, that he will like more than others, because he will identify better with it. The average viewer is like the *favorite* of your story.

When we start writing a script, we have to consider *who it is going to be addressed to*. Is our model spectator a woman or a man? How old is she/he? What is their social status? As you can see, the average viewer has unique characteristics, just like our characters. They may or may not share them. But the moment we think of the viewer, the questions that arise are the same ones that define our characters. And like them, we must consider the average viewer at the beginning of our work. He will serve as the limit to know how far we can go, and what the issues and conflicts are that we will work on in greater depth.

If we do not choose one spectator over another, we will end up walking through a gelatinous structure, wanting to encompass them all, without really touching anyone. It is always better to leave *a single spectator* satisfied than... none at all. And when we have decided that our model viewer is, for example, a single middle-class working man of about 30 years old, we will see that there is more than one that meets these characteristics and we will transmit our message to more than one suitable spectator. If, on the contrary, we don't care if it's a man or a woman, that their age ranges from 20 to 60 years, and we do not pay attention to their social status, no spectator will identify with our history, because when she/he sits in the armchair, she/he does it because she/he wants to feel *special*; he wants to believe that you are telling *him* a story. And he certainly will not like to feel part of an ordinary whole; he already has to deal with that every day of his postmodern life. That is why it is important that you pay attention to this small but essential detail. *Always* choose a viewer and caress him with your story. Give him something to identify with, make him feel unique, and he will thank you with his favorable opinion.

40. Reality exceeds fiction by far

In order to understand this point quickly, a very clear example will be set:

Not long ago, a man managed to get inside the British Queen's bedroom without being seen, heard or discovered. Only when he touched her shoulder and the queen shrieked, did the guards notice that something was wrong.

Now... If we read the headline of the story in the newspaper and we do not advance in the detailed explanation of the facts, we might simply say *'what a good idea for a movie...'* and we begin to write down the details of what will become a script later, in what way will we tell it? We'll probably end up writing a James Bond film, where the character has the mission to get inside the queen's room, and he spends two hours of the film overcoming obstacles at gunfire, blowing half the set and kissing beautiful women, don't we? This would be a promising story, which would have a fair number of viewers, and that could be perfectly plausible and interesting. But, if instead of writing this story, we decide to read the description of the newspaper to write a script that is as true to reality as possible, what we will get as a result will be a failure. Notice why.

It turns out that this man, a thief perhaps, or someone who was simply bored, had been plotting his strategy for some time. He had studied the interiors through guided visits, analyzed the changes of guards, and when the time came, he climbed a lateral vine, waited for the exact moment of the change of guard, entered a window just in time not to be seen, walked by the correct corridors always in the precise moments, and was inside the room in 20 minutes. Consider this story and try to figure out in which fictional universe it would work, without boring or disappointing viewers.

But, why does this happen, if when the news came out in the newspaper it caught the attention of thousands of people who spoke about the event for several days? Why would it not work on the big screen? And the answer lies in the title of the point in question: *reality exceeds fiction by far*. This story, as it happened in reality, *has no conflict*; and that is precisely why people were surprised. A fact like that supposes a great number of obstacles to overcome, and if the man managed his task without problems, we accepted it *because it was real*. But the script is a *creation* that *does not work without conflicts*, because it is not interesting.

On the other hand, there is also the case of *coincidences*. In real life, we accept coincidence because we cannot control it, or understand it. If, for example, we go down the street thinking about someone we have not seen for a long time, and suddenly we meet him, we will be surprised, and we will laugh at the anecdote. But if this happens in a movie, it will not be plausible. These kinds of coincidences are not allowed in a film. (Note that this case is not like the one that was already analyzed for objects and/or casual characters. In that case, they *do not participate in the dramatic action*, unlike this case, in which *they do*.) All viewers know that coincidences are only allowed in reality, and will not allow a scriptwriter to use them, instead of giving a coherent explanation that justifies the action. In fiction, the viewer wants clear answers. And he will be offended if we do not give them to him. The last thing we want is to have offended viewers, right? Especially after the hard work we did to get our idea on the big screen. Be careful with ideas that have *no conflicts* and with *coincidences* in scripts. Always try to work with hard-to-reach goals and always explain to the viewer what he wants to know, even if you only do it at the end of the story.

41. Do not fall in love with a shot or idea

It often happens that scripts are triggered from an epiphany. Suddenly, we see a scene clearly in our mind, with all the necessary characters already confronted, each with a particular goal different from the other, well opposed, and so on. We even imagine the stage and we even think about the music. And it usually happens that the idea has so much weight that it leads us to write a ton of material as if by magic.

But sometimes, something happens that we understand as our brain playing tricks on us: when we start writing the script from our epiphany, we go through different paths, we make our characters overcome obstacles, and suddenly we realize that the story took a completely unexpected turn. It is common for this to happen because this is a script we write out of *inspiration*, not out of *discipline*, in which we rarely consider the plot outline, or treatment, etc. Many times, we do not even know where we are going with what we write, we simply let ourselves be carried away by our magic. Then we get to the middle of the story and we see that it's going through a path that has little to do with our original idea. And we become unbearably melancholic: *'Poor epiphany, it was the whisper of an angel, and now I'm abandoning it.'* And we say, *'Impossible! I must retrace my steps to wherever the story began to be diverted and resume from there.'* We do not consider as a valid option the fact of *discarding that idea* that took us on this exciting road, making us forget the world and ourselves. And we force and force and force the story, erasing and writing again to fit everything, even if nothing is interesting anymore but the original idea. A shame.

You must know now, before your epiphany takes you by surprise, that *nothing in a script is imperative; everything is disposable.* Even if what we throw away is the very promoter idea that got us travelling. The starting point can serve as purpose only for that: *to be a starting point.* Inspiration and talent speak a language we do not know. We are a simple channel through which they flow freely. Only discipline, and perhaps these secrets, can achieve a little orientation for such a torrent. Keep them present for those times when you feel crazy, and do not be discouraged. By now you will have seen that there are more solutions than you thought for those problems that seemed crystallized and unavoidable.

42. *'This is a bad idea; it has already been done'* is not always so. An original twist can become a new story.

How many times have you felt the frustration that every idea that comes to your mind was done before? And for your sad security, these lines must confess that *they are*. Almost everything has been done already. But, wait! Do not jump from the balcony yet! This book is a magician galley, from which much more than rabbits and pigeons come out.

Remember that in cinema *what* is told is not so important. *How* it's told is much more relevant. Therein lies the difference. It may be that in cinema everything is told, but what is not true is that everything has already been told… *in every possible way*! But sssshhh…. Don't say it out loud, or the viewer will hear it.

When we speak of giving an original twist, we are referring precisely to that: to taking a story, whatever that is, and telling it *in a different way*. How? With these examples: changing the point of view, turning a secondary character into a protagonist, making new objects and/or characters appear, changing the scenario, transforming the genre, locating the story at another time in the historical timeline, etc., etc., etc.! Imagine if we take only *one* story and we modify only *one* of the examples each time. We will have at least six new stories to tell. And bearing in mind that these are some of the thousands of possible examples, and that we are talking about a single story. Multiply each example by all the stories already told. Do you think now there is nothing new to tell? Exciting, right?

43. Be careful with the timing of your story. Consider the average time of writing: a year. The average time of production: another year. And the average time till the premiere: another year. Three years from your original idea.

This is a little-known fact, which leads to discarding many excellent scripts due to the simple fact that they have gone out of style. You, as a screenwriter, must keep these times in mind before even thinking about developing an idea. It will save you a lot of valuable time. But beware, it is not being suggested that you abandon your idea, only to be *aware* of the historical time in which it develops.

There are *themes* that are *eternal*, as we have seen above in these lines. Love, revenge, the processes of childhood and adolescence, deceit, obsession, etc. There are other themes that only belong to *certain periods*, which work as fashions. Examples of these topics may be: a newspaper story, a family anecdote, a political conflict, etc. These themes can lead to great ideas and then be turned into big scripts, but they will not catch the attention of the viewer if we try to surprise him with something that was relevant three years ago and was not mentioned again after it went out of style. It doesn't mean that you should think of another idea. What is suggested is that you keep your idea but *place an eternal theme* in the background. Is that clear?

We have, for example, the murder of some young man who resisted a robbery. A classic these days. Telling that story can be very interesting today as you write it. But from now to three years, when it actually appears in cinemas, we will not know what will have happened with security, nor how many other attempts at theft will perhaps attract the interest of the viewer more than your story. We will be risking a lot. On the other hand, if you use that background story as a subplot, choose one of the eternal themes, let's say 'revenge', and develop your whole story by taking *that theme* more into account than the story itself, it will cease to be anchored to a certain historical time, and it will become eternal; because regardless of whether your story is about a murder, or a robbery, or a rape, that has occurred in a given time; revenge is a theme of all times. And then you can continue to tell the story you had in mind from the beginning, but it will have more chances to be enjoyed when you get to the big screen, and your time will have been worth the effort. By the way, you will be closer and closer to turning your artistic work into a classic of all times.

Comments that promise failures

Here are just a few of the most common examples of those ideas that look great but have nothing to do with an epiphany. Sometimes we think that an idea that was successful in one format, can be successful in any other, as has been seen in the case of adaptations. We also believe that if a piece of news in the newspaper was famous, it can be transferred to the cinema. And we even have the illusion that a great idea will always end in a great script. Unfortunately, even though this book offers a lot of solutions, some results are not always as favorable as we want. And many times, no matter how much one feels the need to encourage others in any endeavor they wish to carry out, one of the best ways to do this is to prevent them from walking through a few embarrassing paths. Again, it is worth clarifying that not all bad ideas end in bad scripts, those are just the most well-known cases. It is critical that you know them to be aware of what you are risking.

44. 'What if I take this short that won three awards and make it a feature?'

This idea, which many consider *original*, is present in the minds of almost all the screenwriters who have won awards with their shorts. And it is logical, because they believe that as they have conquered the contest judges and the audience in that way, they can do it again. The problem comes when they think they can do it... *with the same idea*. A short that has won several awards will hardly obtain the same results as a feature film. When we analyzed the different durations of the films at the beginning of this book, they showed the clear differences they present, and why it is important to choose one over another based on the type of idea that we have in mind.

The short film has the *unique* characteristics of presenting few characters, a single conflict and, often, a twist. With those details well worked out, it's usually enough for the short to draw some attention. But that *does not mean* that the same will be enough to draw attention to a *feature*. Even if when we try to stretch a medium-length film to a feature it ends up becoming chewing gum, imagine what will happen with a short. The short film can act as a *trigger* for a feature film, but it will hardly do so as an adaptation. Because even if you add more characters, develop new conflicts and give rise to subplots, you'll probably have something new completely different from your original idea, in which case it will be worth the risk. But if you have in mind that what you want is to *adapt* the short, what will happen is what was mentioned as a warning in lines above: you will try by all means to make the idea present in your feature film and you will be forcing the pieces to fit into a disastrous puzzle.

Remember that luck favors those who work in a disciplined way. The more you know about your profession, the greater your chances of success. That's why it's good to know that sometimes, what seems like a great original idea, has already passed through the minds of those who came before you. Analyze these cases so that your work has as few surprises as possible, and you can create something new with tools that you know and handle.

45. 'Last night I had a great dream. I'm going to write a script.'

Dreams in the cinema are *too* dangerous because they have a *logic of their own* that has nothing to do with the fictional world in which it unfolds. After reading all these lines, you will already have understood that the cinema has tools and resources that are its own and are the most recommended to work in this medium, as they better enhance your creativity.

When we get into the universe of dreams, in general we believe that we can adapt them to the cinema because every time we remember one, *we do it like a succession of facts that are presented illogically, but that our brain is in charge of organizing*. The problem is that our brain organizes what it interprets based on facts that *each one* lived and that are *only* logical *in our brain*. Notice what happens when you tell someone what you dreamed about: you explain the facts as you order them in your memory, but your listener never finishes capturing the whole of it, and in general, it does not seem so fascinating to him.

Dreams have a *time* and *space* that work in a completely different way from that of cinema; in fact, it is one of the characteristics that makes them so wonderful. But, just as there are resources that work in theater or on television, but that do not work in movies, the same happens with dreams. When in a dream we walk through a place that suddenly becomes another, and then another, and people appear and disappear, and it is day, then night, etc., we understand that as *normal* because it is a dream and dreams don't need coherent or logical explanation. Everything seems extremely casual and we do not care what we see because, like coincidences in life, *we cannot control them in our dreams either*.

But cinema *needs* explanation; and if we want to adapt a dream we will fail because, to do so, we have to remove all the characteristics that made it interesting in the first place: we have to order their time, anchor their space, and explain the facts so that viewers can understand them. It does not mean that it is *impossible* to take a dream to cinema; there are hundreds of cases. But most of them move away from the mass audience; indeed, they hardly ever consider them of vital importance. If you only want to make art, you can try it through a dream told in the cinema. But if you want to *convey* something through your art and reach *as many people as possible*, then we suggest you take this idea with you, and analyze all the similar cases you know, so that, once again, you can consciously choose the best way to achieve it, and not become a simple victim, frustrated by an incomprehension which stemmed from your own innocence.

General Genres

Cinema has always been characterized by grouping its films into genres. Not that this was decided from the beginning, but at a certain point, theorists began to notice that there were patterns that categorized films according to their ways of dealing with the story. Thus, genres were born and, since then, there have been so many studies that today it is practically impossible to avoid the placement of a film within a genre.

On the other hand, since the fight in cinema today is carried out in order to obtain the great prize of originality, filmmakers have learned to mix genres like magic potions, to obtain new strategies of war that conquer the spectator. That is the reason why it has been decided to deepen them here. You have probably already read hundreds of books mentioning many types of various genres. It is not the intention of these lines that you experience a *déjà vu*. Rather, what is proposed here is that you can quickly recognize what the specific characteristics of each and their most common faults are, so that you can also consider yourself a magician, and you can fill your cupboards with vials containing the ingredients necessary for originality.

Mixing genres is not a crime, nor is it frowned upon by the film industry. Nowadays, it is one of the most used tools, and it would be good if you present yourself on the battlefield on equal terms.

46. The Love Story

This genre is one of the most common and has been present in the cinema since it began to tell stories. Even if the film relates better to other genres, there is always a time when love comes to light. This happens because, in order to create a film that has a good structure, it has already been seen here that there must be a strong network of personal interrelations. And, in general, it happens that one of those connections is of loving nature. This does not mean that love should express itself as couple's love; there is also the love of brothers, friends, parents and children, etc. Love is one of the main motivations to unleash the passions of the characters. Almost always there is at least one that bases his goal on love, and that is enough for that ingredient to be present in the formula.

On the other hand, the moments in which love expresses itself in cinema are those that connect in a more direct way a character with the spectator. When we finally manage to reveal the characters' feelings, spectators gain access to a satisfaction that goes beyond whether those feelings are reciprocated or not. All the tension that has been accumulating finally gives way and the viewer gets the maximum identification with the character because he has openly shown his heart.

Now, as a specific genre, the love story has a beginning, a middle and an end.

At first, the characters in question are presented, at least two, generally opposed in everything: personal characteristics, objectives to be fulfilled, given circumstances, etc. The more opposed they are to each other, the easier it will for them to be attracted, but the harder it will be for them to unite.

Then, the conflicts between two strong and opposing characters arise as if by magic. If we are clear about what each one wants and what their plan to achieve it is, even the dialogues will flow harmoniously. It has already been seen that a good structure leads more comfortably to a good script, and this is no exception to tell a love story.

To get to the end of our story and make it as interesting as possible, we must make our story go in the *opposite* direction. That is, if we have, for example, a story between a woman and a man and we want them to end up together, they must find all possible reasons for being apart, until they realize that their love is stronger. On the other hand, if we want to tell that they do not belong together, throughout the film they will have to be together many times, so that both understand that although they tried everything, their destiny is not to be together. This is one of the most important characteristics of the love story, and rarely fails if it is well used. It would be good if you as a screenwriter know from the beginning if your characters *will end up together or not*, because that will help you drive them all the time down the opposite path.

Love is one of the *Eternal Themes*, since it has always been present in human life. And over centuries, instead of clearing up and becoming more common, it seems that it becomes more and more complicated and all the time new and interesting ways to face it arise.

As no one is exempt from living a love story of some kind at some point in their life, it turns out that this genre is, moreover, one of the most seen in the history of cinema, and it is the group that most classics fall into. It is also, of course, one of the most difficult to achieve, due to the competition it proposes.

Examples of those who have managed to rely on a strong script, capable of convincingly thrilling viewers are:

- *'French Kiss'*, written by Adam Brooks, from 1995.
- *'Amélie'*, written by Guillaume Laurant and Jean-Pierre Jeunet, from 2001.
- *'The Notebook'*, written by Jan Sardi, based on the novel by Nicholas Sparks, from 2004.

47. The most common flaws in the love story

It often happens that we begin to write the love story and we focus our attention on the central conflict of the film, but we forget other things that are also very important. Let´s see how.

For example, we introduce two characters that are attracted to each other, but we know that we have to achieve a certain number of obstacles to make our story longer and interesting; especially *long*, because in general we believe that we will not get to cover the two hours of film we need only with a love story (and you are not so mistaken if you think that, since no love story covers the entire interest rate that the viewer requests). So, we spend all our time finding those *conflicts,* and it is precisely here where love stories fail: instead of paying attention to *personal interrelations*, we look for ways to make our conflicts more and more interesting, until we end up forcing them. The fact is that this happens because conflicts *arise* from interrelationships, *not the other way around.*

If we fail to build the characters that surround our protagonists, in a short time we will run out of ideas. Secondary characters help to guide the central history because you, as a skilled screenwriter, must build them in such a way that they *oppose to the main ones* and *also to each other.* Remember that all the characters in your story *must have a clear and different objective* from the rest. Even if you choose to carry forward a single point of view, it will be necessary for the secondary characters to *influence* the lives of the principals, to make them hesitate through example and dialogue. The network of interrelations is fundamental in the love story.

The other factor that generally leads to the failure of this genre is to take the characters from the beginning by the path they will end up transiting at the end. If you introduce two characters that meet, attract to each other, communicate perfectly, have a couple of differences but that are not relevant enough to separate them, remain together, and end up together, the viewer -if he has not fallen asleep by the final credits- will remain wondering where that conflict ended that promised to take him to walk through a world full of emotions and feelings. Always remember to direct your characters on paths that only lead to the end that you want because they have proven to be exactly the *opposite* of what they were looking for.

48. Action movies

This genre is preferred by producers because, in general, it does not matter too much if the script is good. It has a visual appeal so imposing that it catches the attention of the viewer even if the story they are telling is the most predictable and boring of all.

However, you do not want to be a mediocre scriptwriter, right? You want to know how to tell a good action story, because what you want is to stand out from the rest, making your ideas an art, right? Then watch closely.

In the genre of action, we find a rude and sulfuric character who is presented with a specific goal -usually initiated by an evildoer that provokes him to obtain some kind of revenge-, and so, to achieve this, he must undergo a series of obstacles that the antagonist cleverly places in his path; not a single path, of course: our protagonist must destroy half a city, get rid of the chief of police, be part of a chase, solve puzzles and overcome his treacherous fear of heights.

In the genre of action, usually, the main character is motivated to fulfill his goal by a *double initiative*. That is, the evildoer is not only putting at risk mankind by means of a bomb that he has hidden but has also studied his opponent and knows his weak point, generally related to some member of his family, whom he threatens to provoke the protagonist. The bad character of the action genre has a *passionate* relationship with the main character. He doesn't want *just anyone* to stop him. He wants *that particular one* who got him arrested once, or who killed a member of his family in self-defense, to look for him. The antagonist's act of vengeance is personal, and all his actions usually have that motivational base.

Since what was mentioned in the previous paragraph is what happens in most action films, for it to be interesting from the script, we must seek originality in the specific resources of the genre. How? We can change the film's point of view and respect all these characteristics, but making the viewer identify, for example, with *the bad guy*. How do we achieve this? By carefully explaining *his* motive for revenge. We must show the viewer that this character *became bad* because someone committed a terrible injustice against him and the case has never been solved, so he was forced to take the law in his own hands. In addition, we can help the viewer's identification by showing that the good guy is not as good as he appeared to be.

Another way to create an original action script is to look for novel and unusual scenarios that help visually. You may have noticed how many movies have the same plot, but only their scenarios are modified. If you get your scenario to be unique, you will have one more factor of interest in the viewer.

Do you realize, writer friend? The script has its own magic. The characters, objectives, conflicts, dialogues and so on are tools that will not change the basis of the genre, but they can make it a much more interesting story than a simple succession of explosions and fights. Do not forget to also place a little love story to spice up the narrative.

As an example, we are going to pay tribute to the sagas, which in general turn out to be second and even hurried third parts of original box office successes. But every so often you get one that is worth sitting down to marathon an entire afternoon:

- *'The Bourne Identity'* saga, written by Tony Gilroy, from the years 2002, 2004 and 2007.
- The *'Lethal Weapon'* saga, written by Shane Black, Jeffrey Boam, Robert Mark Kamen and Channing Gibson, from 1987, 1989, 1992 and 1998.

49. The most common flaws in action movies

Although, as we mentioned, this is the preferred genre of producers, it sometimes happens that, even if we have a good script, it becomes a failure that escapes our hands. In general, this case has to do with bad special effects that cause the viewer to be disappointed and removed from the emotional moment, disbelieving the characters. No matter how many details we include in the script, the visuals will always run over our words, and the worst thing is that we cannot remove all those persecution and fight scenes, because then it would not be an action movie. But, in the meantime, we can see how these films fail from the script, because if they do, and then a bad director comes along, we are doomed.

It has already been said that in action movies there is a bad character that provokes the good one. It happens that many times the bad guy is *wickedly evil*, but he does not have any strong motivation to be so; he's just *the bad guy*. Then our main character is no longer provoked by personal reasons and becomes an altruist who does everything for the good of humanity. Dear screenwriter, I know you can give much more. Look inside your soul and you will find that connection between the protagonist and the antagonist. Find it out and take advantage of it. Note that it is not very difficult to enrich your story.

Remember to place the innocent secondary character too, and also put him/her in the network of interrelations. A few warnings: it's not valid that a character that has nothing to do with the story suddenly appears and gives the protagonist the key that was missing to find the bomb that would destroy the world. Nor are the *listeners* valid, so frequently present in these films that they work as mannequins so that the hero or the bad guy can explain his strategy in a long monologue. And, finally, it is not enough that we have small but exciting obstacles. The main objective of the protagonist must be too strong, since he will put his life at stake to reach it... too many times! Make your antagonist empathic too, let the viewer understand his motivations, even if he does not identify with them. Forget the bad clichés and build the decent characters these lines know you can achieve.

50. The adventure

Adventure movies have as their main characteristic the presentation of stories that occur in *unusual scenarios*, such as jungles, deserts, mountains and galaxies, and that are worked on in a plausible way because this manages to build itself from the *main objective*. Pay attention, Mr. or Mrs. Scriptwriter, because this is a subject that is radically up to you. If you did not have time to understand what was just mentioned, it will be repeated for your benefit: *the verisimilitude of the adventure story is based on the main objective*. That is: it is something that the main character must get that has nothing to do with the *usual*. These objectives are related to discoveries, destructions, manipulations, creations, salvations and so on, from magical coffers, fairy dust, elf-protected coffins, golden fleeces, rings whose power exceeds human knowledge, etc. In short... you may have already understood what kind of films are referred to.

Let's set some examples:

- The complete saga of *'Star Wars'*, by George Lucas, from 1977, 1980, 1983, 1999, 2002, 2005, 2015, 2017, and 2019.
- The complete saga of *'The Lord of the Rings.'*
- *'The Chronicles of Narnia: The Lion, the Witch and the Wardrobe,'* based on the novel by C.S. Lewis, and adapted for the screen by Ann Peacock, Andrew Adamson, Christopher Marcus, and Stephen McFeely, from 2005.

But why is the goal emphasized so much? Because only one objective of these characteristics *justifies* scenarios and characters of this nature. And the *main objective* of a character depends only on you. No member of the film crew can create it so skillfully. If you do not take responsibility, the film will plummet from the moment it is put in the director's hands. A pity, considering that the structure of the genre is based on something so common to you as a goal. Think of something that motivates the characters -that exceeds the limits of human understanding and scientific reason- that is based on magic and can create new and fascinating characters and scenarios to tell the story you want. Do not forget to extract from your cupboard the jars with condiments of love and action, and you will make magic from the mixture of genres.

In the adventure genre, we find a main character who has a very clear objective in his life. For this reason, these heroes are often daring, intelligent and insightful. They are also usually accompanied by some secondary character, some friend, nephew, cousin or robot, almost always smaller in age and size, and more coward, but more prudent. These secondary characters are the ones who often rescue the principal from the problems he gets into.

Another of the typical characteristics of the adventure is the main character's *object of desire*. This has nothing to do with the objective. The goal is the one that causes him to get going and to go through the strange worlds. The object of desire is what moves the hero *back to his home*. Throughout the film, this character crosses a duality between his goal and his object of desire, which make him reconsider his values and his entire life. For more information about this genre and the hero's characteristics, you can dig into 'the hero's journey', clearly explained through simple images you can easily find in the Internet.

51. The most common flaws in adventure

The importance of the objective in this genre has already been made quite clear. We have seen that only if we present a strange objective, which moves away from the human reality, we can carry forward our story in new and different scenarios, with characters that we will never see outside this story; and this happens because the spectator *will never consider an adventure to go through paths that he already knows*.

But what we never ask ourselves is why we choose this genre beyond the possibilities it offers our imagination. While it is very interesting to see how far creativity can go, our film will be quickly forgotten if we do not add the magic dust. What is referred to here is the *social implication* that these films can access, but to which they rarely do.

When we move away from planet Earth to tell a story, in reality what we try to do is seek *new points of view* to know how we can modify a reality that we know, but that does not convince us. Or at least, we should. Because if we only show a new world, which has nothing to do with our reality, the viewer will be very fascinated, but will be able to relate that story little to his own life, and our story will be forgotten the moment he sees the light from the living room again. On the other hand, if we move away from this reality, but we manage to show new life forms that relate to our world, then it will draw the attention of the viewer and he will think '*Ok... if that personage outside the Earth acted that way and obtained results that can be obtained here as well, it may be useful for me to apply it.*' The adventure genre fails from the script when the viewer cannot anchor the film with the facts and decisions of his daily life. It does not fail because it ceases to be interesting; it fails because it is quickly forgotten.

52. The Suspense

Seen and considering that so many secrets have already been revealed for the writing of the film script, it is considered pertinent here to pay homage to the master of the suspense of all time. Ladies and gentlemen, let us warmly welcome Mr. Alfred Hitchcock. Applause! Applause! No one has managed to express the foundations and grounds of suspense like him, so there is no intention here of competing with his talent, but of making it present in our memory. If you are interested in writing suspense, we cannot help but suggest that you lock up a week at home with the blinds down and devote yourself to seeing all of this author's filmography; several times, if you can. But who has such an amount of time today? Do not be discouraged; these lines will simplify your life once more.

Hitchcock has established, in the conversations with François Truffaut that gave rise to the excellent book '*Hitchcock*', three different types of suspense, which are relevant here because they relate *directly* to the script. Pay close attention!

> 1. *The character knows something that the viewer does not know.* Example: The murderer who plans to kill his victim, while posing as good and polite in the eyes of him and the viewer.
> 2. *The character knows the same as the viewer.* Example: The woman who steals money and escapes and neither she nor we know if she is being persecuted.
> 3. *The character knows less than the viewer.* Example: The bomb under the table about to explode, which the viewer is aware of, but the characters are not.

Of course, you only need to read these lines to understand why this classification is said to relate directly to the script. If we, as writers, do not determine from the outset *what point of view* we are going to work on, we will carry forward an untidy film, which will become predictable in most cases. This is not to say that we have to *maintain ourselves all the time* within the same group throughout a film. We can vary as long as we want to convey *surprise, confusion or tension*. Even the suspense film becomes more interesting if we manage to move from one to another at different times, because we will be giving the viewer the possibility of feeling the most different emotions. Know that *this* is precisely the reason why the viewer goes to see a suspense film. He wants to feel everything and wants to play with danger, without risking his own life, of course. And cinema is one of the most effective ways to get what you are looking for.

Now... as you have seen, each of these groups provokes a different emotion.

If we have a character who *knows something that the viewer does not know*, like the example of our 6-year-old boy who crashed the car without the viewer knowing because we have ellipsed it, remember?, questions will be generated in the viewer, and the moment when he discovers the answers will depend on us. And we will use this to provoke *intrigue* and then, *surprise*.

If, on the other hand, the viewer *knows the same thing as the character*, we will make him feel different emotions from the moment the character feels them, because *the equation in the level of knowledge of both causes identification*. Then the viewer will feel tension, intrigue, suspense, surprise and so on, as long as we provoke those emotions in the main character.

Finally, when we want the viewer to feel as much suspense as possible, we must *make the danger our innocent character is facing known*. This case is the most effective to generate suspense but remember that no viewer can endure it for a long time, so it should be applied in small doses.

If we successfully manage to manipulate these groups, we will dominate a range of emotions that we can use at the moment we consider more appropriate. And it is also worth clarifying that these formulas are applicable to any story, whether we are writing a love story or a horror story. If we consider who knows what and how much each knows, in each story we will have the possibility of accessing more emotions, which will attract more voracious viewers.

53. The most common flaws in suspense

In this genre, what should most concern you is that the viewer *cannot guess the end beforehand*. All the suspense of a film can be sustained as long as we can manipulate the feelings of the audience.

But what are the factors that lead to the spectator's forecast of the end? These have to do with the imbalance between what is *explained* and what is *hidden*; because we have to give enough explanations so that the viewer can understand what the story is about, but we must hide enough for him to become intrigued and tense. It is very difficult to obtain this balance. Many times, we think of lying to the viewer to mislead him, but the lie is not valid for this book. It is one thing for *him* to believe that he is seeing something when in reality *we* are showing him something different; and another very different thing is to lie with non-existent points of view, or, for example, showing him a character that appears at the end out of nowhere, who comes to explain everything, but never appeared before. Do not let yourself be tempted to take the easy way, because you will be lacking respect for the viewer.

There are other ways of getting the mystery to be preserved and have to do with a point that has already been discussed here, which relates to *the questions that the viewer asks himself*. It has already been seen that for questions to arise in the mind of the viewer, they must first do so in the mind of the screenwriter; and it has already been suggested that you *write down these questions, since if you do not, you risk forgetting them*. The moment the viewer asks himself the first question, he will unleash in his mind a list of possible options for answering it; and if between them is the end of your film, he will have guessed it. It is up to you to manipulate those responses as skillfully as you can. We can enjoy an action or love movie, even if the end is predictable, but it is the *uncertainty* that makes us enjoy a suspense film, so always keep this in mind if you want to dedicate yourself to working in this genre.

54. The Horror

This genre was created from the disconformity of the human being with scientific experiments. As science progressed and made new discoveries, there were some scientists who considered themselves all-powerful, able to solve the mysteries of science and control life and death. These films then emerged to critique these narcissistic minds and used to be based on scientific experiments that failed and gave rise to monsters with a pure, instinctive will. These monsters became uncontrollable and the scientist was forced to step down from his pedestal, ashamed of the irreparable damage that his creation had done. For a closer approach to what is being told, see *'Frankenstein,'* written by Garrett Fort and Francis Edward Faragoh, based on the novel by Mary Shelley, from 1931.

As these films play with the manipulation of those virtues that are proper to nature, and that escape human understanding, they create unrealistic scenarios that become plausible in the same way as in the case of adventure: fundamental conflicts are built on a basis that goes beyond human reason.

Over time, imagination has given rise to increasingly complex and fascinating creatures, who have achieved success on the big screen thanks to, fortunately for the ignorant scriptwriter, a large chart of novel visual elements.

But it is important for you as a writer to know that *these monsters are also characters*, and that, as such, have to present *unique characteristics, clear objectives, and given circumstances*. It would also be good to consider some of the wildcards of the genre, such as the famous innocent girl in danger, who gives deafening shrills, a hero who can beat the beast, and scenarios based on superstitions, dark legends, black magic and nightmares. You can add that the hero falls in love with the girl, or better, that the monster does, and then have a love story; you can also cause the monster to destroy the whole city so that there is nothing lacking in action; and, why not, perhaps a good deal of intrigue and suspense. Remember that since this is also a very visual genre, the excesses of blood in the descriptions will be of great help.

Here there is another saga worth paying tribute to:

- The *'Scream'* saga, written by Kevin Williamson and Ehren Kruger, from 1993, 1997, and 2000. A good option to study scripts that take advantage to the fullest not only this genre, but also of action, suspense and the love story.

55. The most common flaws in horror films

While it is common knowledge that flaws in this genre have more to do with visual issues than with structure, there are some things that the screenwriter must consider, which are *their* responsibility. We cannot just sit back and wait for a director to come and make our story a success, because then why did we think about this genre in the first place. We must add our grain of sand so that the art department does not take all the credit.

The most common failings of horror writers, aside from relying too heavily on the skills of the film crew, have to do with the construction -or non-construction- of the main characters. We think more or less of the hero, the innocent girl, but what about our monster? We must pay attention to him too and build him much more than an unpleasant appearance.

Our monster must be empathic; that is, the viewer must be able to connect with him, if not from identification, at least from the understanding of his discomfort. Our monster must feel that he has been wronged; must feel the frustration of having an entire society against him that wants to eliminate him when in principle it was them who created him; he must feel discriminated against and act accordingly. The interesting thing about these monsters is that we can equip them with *spirit*, give them a *soul*. We are the scriptwriters, right? We can do whatever we want with our characters. Blood and fear will continue to bathe the big screen, and we will enchant the viewer, who will not only take a good dose of emotions but will be surprised by the unexpected depth of the story. Always keep these details in mind; they are very common flaws, perfectly avoidable, especially for a creative scriptwriter like yourself.

56. Science fiction

Science fiction has the characteristic of being based on *social laws*, which the writer is responsible for skillfully misrepresenting, reversing or reinventing. Films of this genre are not understood as a whole if one does not take into account the *context* in which they were created, since its main objective is to criticize those laws and social customs that led, over the years, to wars, civil conflicts, repressions and punishments.

Social malaise is usually based on power games, carried out by greedy and ambitious humans; and by an ignorant dominated mob, who tragically suffer the consequences of the battles between the powerful ones.

Science fiction serves to bring awareness to the masses from a social critique that relates to this problem. How does it do it? *Exaggerating* those customs that are *implicit* in a society, which serve the dominant ones to exert their power. That is, it builds a universe where *these customs become law*. Then we find worlds where free verbal and artistic expression is *prohibited*; schools where children *are required* to write their homework using only a few idiomatic tools, and they can only refer to specific subjects; cities where laughter *is not allowed* and where police violence is not only authorized but *compulsory*; places where reading books is *prohibited*, etc.

In science fiction a character almost always appears who finds all these absurd laws and tries to reverse the situation of tyranny in which he is. This gives rise to other characters such as the police, the friend who tries to get him to reason and so on.

Because the viewer is aware that the universe of science fiction is unreal, since he would never authorize a level of injustice so evident in real life, it allows the use of scenarios and unreal characters, which will form part of the plausible without problems. This is not obligatory, but it is worth the effort to take advantage of them, because they will give rise to more creative and novel ideas that will not have to do with the story itself, but with the way in which it is told.

Excellent examples of this genre are:

- *'A Clockwork Orange'*, by Stanley Kubrick, 1971, based on the novel by Anthony Burgess.
- *'Planet of the Apes'*, written by Michael Wilson and Rod Serling, 1968, based on the novel by Pierre Boulle.
- *'Fahrenheit 451'*, by François Truffaut, from 1966, based on Ray Bradbury's novel.

57. The most common flaws in science fiction

In order to successfully carry out this genre, it is imperative that *studies be done of the society to which the film is directed.* It is not the spectator who must enter into code with our idea, but it is *we* who must adapt to his customs. This is one of the reasons why these films sometimes fail. We try to convey a message to generate awareness in the viewer and, as we have not analyzed the *proper* characteristics of that society in depth, we find ourselves messing up in front of an audience that does not understand what we want to say. And the fault will be ours alone, since we have not done our job properly. *The inquiry about the model viewer* of our idea is more important here than in any other genre, and that requires not only virtue but also discipline.

58. The Fantastic

This genre also gets involved with those things that are mysterious or inexplicable to human reason. Usually, these stories go hand in hand with adventure and/or suspense. They serve for the development of those minds that do not find satisfaction in reality. The screenwriters of the fantastic believe in underworlds, supernatural beings, and the existence of life on other planets, parallel realities and travel in time.

Fantastic films work on all these characteristics in a manner similar to *empirical research*; and often have as their *aim the social critique* of closed and limited minds, which do not accept a point of view different from their own, and which are incapable of seeing beyond their own noses.

As a classic feature of this genre we have a character who has learned that someone witnessed something supernatural and begins collecting evidence, conducting interviews, and recording events from all possible rational angles until he is so involved in the subject that our strange character ends up getting angry and gives him all the evidence he was looking for, but in the worst possible way. That, in the case that the strange is *bad*. Because as the fantastic has no limits, suddenly we can meet strange *good beings* that help in the investigation.

These films usually have three types of possible endings, which a good man named Todorov investigated and classified in a more than eloquent way in his paper 'Introduction to Fantastic Literature':

1. The supernatural exists. (The author calls it: *Fantastic*) Example: Vampires, werewolves, superheroes, etc.
2. There is no supernatural. (Then it qualifies as: *Strange*) Example: It was not a UFO, but an escape of green gas. She was not a virgin who cried blood, but some children wanting to get attention, etc.
3. It is unknown if the supernatural exists. (It is said to be: *Amazing strange*)

The fantastic works as a pendulum, going between the rational and the supernatural all the time. And in general, we don't learn the truth of the mysteries until the end. It is very difficult for a viewer to guess the end of this film, because the rules of credibility are being built on the go. Or at least that's what he believes. Mr. Scriptwriter, please try to decide well in advance what is going to happen in your story; it is important that *you do know* the end, and that you hide it from the viewer to give more suspense to the investigation.

Of the three possible endings, you will have noticed that the most interesting one is the third. It is always good to leave some –yes, yes... some– unanswered questions in this genre, because the truth is that *nobody knows if these things really exist or not*. We can believe that they do or they don´t, but we are always going to have to leave confirmation to faith.

Many of the cases that end up as suggested by the *first option* usually have a format similar to that of the documentary, with interviews and reports and archival material that give more weight to the facts, so that the viewer believes them.

For their part, the films that end up based on the *second option* are also based on investigation, but their resolution ends up being under the explanation of something perfectly real, though strange to ordinary people, e.g.., factories, laboratories, etc.

Research into the fantasy genre is a classic, but it is not a law. There are many films of this genre that are carried out on their own, sometimes we can even have the view of the supernatural being. Remember that this genre has very few rules, which serve as the basis for all that different and novel universe that you will invent; but since you will invent it, remember to respect it. Otherwise you will lose the plausible that it has taken you so much work to build.

Examples of the fantastic are:

- *'Underworld'*, written by Danny McBride, from 2003.
- *'Superman'* (in any of its versions)

Examples of the strange are:

- *'The Phantom of the Opera'* (in any of its versions)
- *'The Village'*, by M. Night Shyamalan, from 2004.

Examples of the amazing strange are:

- *'Unbreakable'*, by M. Night Shyamalan, from the year 2000.
- *'Phenomenon'*, written by Gerald Di Pego, from 1996.

59. The most common flaws in the fantastic

As we have seen, in the fantasy genre, the first thing we see are beings that have the main characteristic of being *weird*. As the story progresses, we will learn more details about them, which will lead us progressively towards the moment in which the screenwriter decides on one of the three possible endings.

This gives rise to two types of common flaws: the first has to do with a carefree scriptwriter who writes his story without knowing where he is going with it; that is, he does not know how it will end until the very end. The other flaw has to do with a screenwriter who, even taking into account where he wants to go, lets the story get away from his hands and ends up choosing the hateful *open end*, which has nothing to do with *ambiguity*; this screenwriter leaves the viewer with important questions in his head, which he never answers. Both cases are perfectly avoidable if you take the trouble to analyze your idea in a disciplined way. At this point you have the necessary and sufficient tools to do it.

60. Crime and investigation

The news related to criminology were always the ones that most attracted the attention of human beings. It is not surprising that cinema has set eyes on them at the very moment it realized the amount of audience they could attract.

At first, the films were based on a particular case in which the investigator, the false suspect, the murderer and the victim were always present. In this genre, a secondary character also appears who has some key data for the resolution of the mystery: maybe it is a fundamental witness who refuses to give testimony for fear of getting into trouble; maybe it is an expert chemist in a certain substance that is present at the scene of the crime, etc. Many crime stories are based on real facts, which is why they try to maintain the greatest neatness and relation with reality possible.

Examples of classic crime stories are:

- 'Seven', from 1992, written by Andrew Kevin Walker.
- 'The Bone Collector', written by Jeremy Iacone, from 1999.
- 'The silence of the lambs', from 1991, written by Ted Tally, based on the novel by Thomas Harris.

As time went by, the *film noir* emerged, where crime and investigation were also present, but two almost essential new characters appeared and scenarios that became classics of the genre. One of the characters is the *detective*, who, although already present in the classic crime story, is given much more importance here, since he is an outcast, perhaps an alcoholic, who must investigate a certain crime at the same time he is faced with an existential exploration of his own life; he no longer knows if he wants to continue in that profession, but ends up accepting the case because he is always the most indicated one; not to mention, of course, that perhaps the killer has some personal long standing conflict with him. The other character that appears in this type of crime story is the *femme fatale*; she is a mysterious, confident, superhot woman who can appear both to help the demotivated detective and to collaborate with the murderer. It is a dual character that is always suspected to be the killer, but the most important thing is that it is strong and sometimes it is the one that carries the story forward.

With respect to the classic scenarios of the film noir, these are the alleys of the suburbs of the cities, at night, and with rain. This last factor led to the cliché that the detective is always wearing a raincoat.

Examples of film noir are:

- *'The Black Dahlia'*, based on the novel by James Ellroy, adapted for the screen by Josh Friedman, 2006.
- *'Sin City'*, written by Frank Miller, from 2005.

Often, what makes a crime story more interesting is that the *protagonist is the criminal*. This is because, in general, we do not know much about this character, since all the time he hides from the police; but it is always interesting for the viewer to get inside his twisted mind. Many times, as spectators, we receive information about them, perhaps we see how they murder their victims, but it is rarely *he* who carries the story forward. It is risky to work on this point of view because it is difficult for the viewer to *identify with a killer* (because as you know, the viewer usually identifies with the protagonist), but if you look inside your memory, you will remember some case and see how interesting it is. And as a scriptwriter, it is recommended that you keep this detail in mind to add interesting condiments to your story that will motivate the viewer to stop by the movie theater.

61. The most common flaws in crime and investigation stories

The worst and most common mistake that crime and investigation scriptwriters make is not about character building, conflict, or scenario. The most terrible and annoying of all common mistakes is to *invent a character who appears five minutes before the end to justify the whole story,* either because he is the mysterious killer, or because he has a key secret that was never spoken about, and so on. The saddest thing of all is that, in general, the scriptwriter who commits these acts of heresy, *had been aware of them since he began to write his story!* And as he knows that there will be no way for the spectator to guess his end, since he *will never give a single clue,* he walks through the story quietly and in a carefree manner. The spectator suspects of all the characters, draws conclusions that he discards after five minutes, is fascinated with the story, stays on the edge of the armchair, believing that he has been fortunate to enjoy the most talented scriptwriter in the world, and suddenly... plaff! A puddle of mud. It turns out that three teenagers appear, who do not even live in the neighborhood where the murder took place, one of them had stolen the gun from his father, and escaped, and just passed through the town, where the victim was just passing by, got scared and killed him.

How much disappointment the viewer will feel. He will never want to hear about you again.

We can have all kinds of flaws, common to all genres, such as insufficient development of a character, generating a weak network of interrelations, misuse of scenarios; but even all of them are preferable to this disastrous option. Please, save the viewer the annoyance and let him know from the beginning that your end will be mediocre; or make good use of your talent as you know you can.

62. The Comedy

This has been and will always be the most complicated genre to carry out successfully. When we, as screenwriters, sit in front of the computer ready to write, for example, a love story, we know what the things that are going to attract the attention of the viewer are. We know which will be the moments in which he is going to be moved, which the ones when he is going to relax, in which he is going to tense. Maybe our story doesn't get to be the most interesting, or a film that goes down in history as a classic. But the moment the viewer sits in the movie theater, guessing when he'll be more prone to feeling certain emotion will not be difficult. The same thing happens with an action movie, or a horror film. But when it comes to a comedy, predicting what the viewer will feel is harder to achieve.

We might never find two people in the world who feel the same need to laugh at the same joke or gag. What each finds funny depends on their own life experiences, which are unique in each case. You could say that the same thing happens with the rest of emotions, but it is not so; because when one feels, for example, that he has fallen in love, certain events occur that are similar in all people: we want to know if our love is reciprocated, we become nervous in front of that person, our knees tremble, we blush, etc. But when a person tells a joke, we can assume that the listener is going to laugh, but we cannot confirm it until he actually does.

Humor is part of a privileged mind, sufficiently skilled to relate quickly and directly the *topic of conversation* that is being maintained with the *familiar and social context* in which it develops. And not only that, but it also has to parody them or ironize them both enough to make them funny, but not too much, to be understood.

However, it is also true that when you write you have *time* in your favor. That is, you can analyze your characters and the conversations they are having, relate them to the context, and even opt for several different comments to see which one looks better. That is a luxury that cannot be given in real life. So in principle we have a point in our favor.

The comedy also has characteristics that are its own, which help release tensions and achieve a more relaxed audience, with an attitude more prone to laughter. The main character of the most innocent comedy often has *very bad luck*. He tries by all means to get something, but everything seems to be against him; from the scenarios, the other characters, the weather, the objects, the time, etc. He is always in the wrong place at the wrong time.

For this to become more comical, there is always an antagonistic character who, instead of consciously complicating his life as in other genres, opposes him because *luck is always on his side*. On top of the fact that our poor victim has punctured the wheel of his bicycle on a heavily rainy day, the other character passes in a stunning car, very comfortable, and the wheel goes into a bump in front of him and bathes him from top to bottom. As if it was not wet enough already. These types of cases are known as *tragicomedies*. We laugh at the poor character, but his situation is really not funny at all, but rather tragic.

A good example of this case is *'The Full Monty'*, written by Simon Beaufoy, from 1997. Social misfortunes take a group of men to the extreme of striptease to get money. What should be tragic ends up finding a more encouraging point of view.

There is also black humor, in which human disabilities are grossly exalted, even bizarrely.

As an example, we have the parody of *'Scream'*: *'Scary Movie'*, written by Shawn and Marlon Wayans, from the year 2000. Apart from parody itself being a form of comedy, in this case, the humor extends to the bizarre, and one ends up laughing no longer at the parodied film, but at the disgusting things he sees.

On the other hand, there're also comedies that are fun because they work on the nonsense and the absurd. In these comedies, universes are constructed in which things happen that, far from being unrelated to reality, *take advantage of it* to distort it, contradict it or exaggerate it. For example, in a film of this category, we can meet a character who goes to the supermarket and finds it quite logical and normal to buy seven hundred small mayonnaise envelopes, instead of carrying a large jar. At first, this creates doubt in the viewer, but when we see that the character arrives to his house, accommodates the sachets in the refrigerator and simply removes one at random to accompany his meal, then we enter in code with the absurd. But for this to happen, two things have to be considered: the first is that the character must act without any surprise, while those around him must look at him as if he were crazy; the second is that this example is absurd only in a world where there are mayonnaise sachets and where there is the option to buy them, but with different purposes; otherwise, the code won't be understood.

Anyway... comedy deserves a whole book for itself. There are hundreds of studies done that try to explain what the basics and characteristics of laughter are. But the reality is that the mood of the spectator, his life experiences, the context in which the film is carried out and so on are always at stake. There are too many factors that influence so that one can bet in advance if his film is going to be a success or not.

As examples, you can always count on the films by the greatest comedians in History such as Charles Chaplin, the Marx brothers, Woody Allen, etc. Any film by these talented people is worth being studied, because the elements mentioned work perfectly, mixing the ingredients with extreme skill. The good comedian has an extra gift that has nothing to do with the writer's profession. If you feel that you are part of that privileged group, then have faith and simply use the tools presented here to tell stories.

63. The most common flaws in comedy

Since this is the most difficult genre of all, the most common flaws are thousands and very varied. But many times, they have nothing to do with the scriptwriter, but with a connection of random facts and planetary conjugations, which, of course, escape from his hands. It is very difficult to know in advance if a character is going to generate the necessary identification with the viewer to make him laugh. So, when the scriptwriter is finally successful enough to make the viewer fall from his chair because of a laughing fit, this immediately becomes a cliché and reappears not only in the saga of that film, but in many others, which take advantage of it as a wild card. We cannot blame the poor scriptwriter; he doesn't know about the risk involved in writing comedy. The flaws of this genre have to do with writing something that we think is going to be comical, but which in the end is not. And no matter how much more research we do, and famous characters we find throughout history, no matter how much we wish to satisfy the audience, in the end everything will depend on the scriptwriter's natural talent to make the audience laugh, combined with the spectator's optimum state of mind, in a strange viscous and volatile formula.

64. The documentary

The documentary is used to convey information that is drawn directly from reality. We work with long shots to give space location and with close shots to emphasize something specific. But, usually, the shots do not try to say anything by themselves; they are impersonal... This is, without a doubt, a... *big lie!* The fact that someone *tries* to be as impersonal as he can with what he is telling *does not make the point of view disappear*. It will always be *a version of the facts*. This is something that one usually forgets as a viewer, because when we sit in front of a documentary, we believe practically everything that is told to us as if it were the truth. As a spectator, you should always take any information offered by a documentary with some skepticism, especially with those that talk about politics, History, or controversial situations; and as a screenwriter, know that you will have the construction of the story in your favor. Few viewers will question whether your story is related to the true reality or not.

In order for the facts within the documentary to be taken by the viewer as a direct expression of reality, the author often uses the impersonal voice-over to relate what is being viewed, looks for archival material such as newspapers, magazines and newsreels, which he uses as evidence to support what he is saying, and he also uses interviews with people experienced in the field, so that everything he is showing is understood as *filmed reality* and not as *one more fictional story of the pack*. This is the reason why many authors decide to opt for this genre to tell their story, especially if there are political implications in it. The author's intention is to say, *'Something has happened or is happening or is going to happen, and you, not as a spectator, but as a human being, must know it.'* Everything that comes in documentary format will always be loaded with a direct relationship with reality. In addition, this genre is more television than cinematic, so it becomes more massive.

In general, the documentary genre is used to tell things from a real world that the viewer *does not have easy access to*, such as wild animals, the universe, the interior of the human body, History, the true intentions of politicians who hide themselves skillfully under speeches and campaigns, etc.

For its part, there is a variant of the documentary, which is obtained from the mixture of genres, called *false documentary*. In this case, some of the resources mentioned, classic of this genre, are taken to tell a fictional story, in order to make the story more credible for the viewer. The writers who choose to work on the false documentary do so because they have something to say -a point of view on a subject- and want that version of the facts to be interpreted as a *possible truth*. This is usually related to the criticism of some historical fact of Humanity, from which only a certain point of view has been made known, which has been accepted as unique. The false documentary comes to break with this structure and gives the viewer the possibility to build a new version of the facts, or at least to question the previous one.

As the false documentary blends *fiction* with *reality*, the message that is often conveyed by using this resource is that *sometimes the boundary between reality and fiction is a thin line that can be easily corrupted*. Above all, by those who try to conceal certain aspects of reality in order to keep a dominated mass ignorant. The writers try, then, to send a message to these spectators to raise awareness and force them to think how much of what they live is reality and how much is fiction.

One of the greatest examples of false documentary is:

- *'No men beyond this point'*, from 2015, written and directed by Marc Sawers.

The great thing about this false documentary is that it uses every documentary tool -interviews with specialists, newspapers, etc.-, to talk about something that is not only fiction but impossible in the world as we know it today. A great movie to understand how a documentary is made.

65. The most common flaws in the documentary

The most common flaws, when it comes to the documentary, are of two types:

The first has to do with the obvious relationship between gender and reality. The flaw appears when we do not carry out sufficient prior investigation and end up taking for granted events that never took place; or we misinterpret the little information that we access to, we forget that it belongs to *one more mere point of view*, and we understand it as the *only truth*, giving rise to a poor documentary.

The other flaw has to do with basing a documentary on facts that are *easily accessible* to the viewer, as we will probably end up facing an audience that knows more about the subject than we do and it will be embarrassing to appear in the newspaper the next day, a critic who points to us with his accusing finger and sends us to the principal's office for not having done our homework correctly. Either way will annoy the viewer and, considering that this genre is the most televised of all those mentioned, probably whoever is watching will use his big toe to feed his frantic addiction to zapping.

My mind is blank!

In this part of the book those secrets that make our talent stay in line throughout the whole trip that involves the writing of a feature film will be announced.

From the time we begin to write until we finish, all kinds of different emotions pass through our body. Sometimes we feel that we are inspired and write forty pages; other times we get frustrated and spend hours sitting at the computer with our fingers on the keyboard without being able to move them; we go through periods when we think we have made a mistake and wish to work from 9 to 18 with that wonderful salary guaranteed at the end of the month; perhaps we cry, believing that no one will ever understand our point of view; and even go as far as to engage in deep conversations with each of the small insects that decide to join us in our odyssey. And yes, dear screenwriter. The truth is that sometimes we spend months and even years writing the same feature film, which means we should expect to feel all these emotions at some point. From this part, we cannot promise that everything is going to turn out as expected, but you can *prevent* some small things that will try to steal your mood throughout the development of your precious work.

It turns out to be that there are several secrets, some that you have already had the opportunity to read here before, others that you will find out later, that can make your frustrations become full pages and your misunderstandings become as transparent to the viewer as clear waters. And the best thing is, if you turn these secrets into discipline, you will never have to deal with those discomforts again.

Come this way... behind this curtain... you will find a world of magical alchemical solutions!

I don't know how to start

66. Nothing begins. Everything is *'In Media Res'*.

When we think of writing a story, whatever it is, it's because we've come up with an *idea*. Whether we imagine two characters in conflict, or we clearly see a strange and striking scenario in our mind, or we are presented with a resolution to a conflict that we are not yet clear about, it is always good to take note of those ideas, so we can calmly sit to develop them later.

We have seen that a good conflict is usually generated *from* well-structured characters, to whom we ascribe age, gender, social status and strong and clear goals, different between them and, at best, opposite to each other. But if we want to introduce each one of them, where they live, how they talk and so on, without presenting the conflict yet, we will most likely have to resort to verbal torrents and explanatory dialogues whose sole function is to make the characters known, but which do not have any dramatic importance. This makes us quickly lose interest in telling a story. We will get bored and our whole visualization will be occupied with the image of the spectators falling into a deep sleep before the end of the initial sequence of titles. But do not worry, Mr. Scriptwriter, there is a solution.

We can write a story in the best way that it seems to us, and then *reorder it* for the viewer. That is, if instead of presenting the characters in their daily activities, we get into the conflict as if we were writing a short film, we will immediately see them in action and that will make us visualize their ways of moving, talking, and even imagine the things they do by reflection. This is what the expression *'In Media Res'* means. Imagining the characters in action is always the best alternative for movies. Action is image and film is image, which makes them both perfectly compatible.

Once we write the conflict scene, we will magically begin to think about the *moments* that took place *prior* to that action and it will be much easier to present our characters because we have already seen them in action. Preparing the clues that will lead to that first turning point will be easier, and the viewer will never know where we have started. He will only see the ordered story and will be carried away by these signs believing that you, as a screenwriter, perfectly mastered your talent to tell stories.

67. Obliged questions of the spectator (none must be answered immediately)

We have already seen that the presentation of a conflict unleashes some questions in our mind that we must take note of, since they will be the ones that the spectator will ask later. These questions are of the following kind:

- Who is this subject?
- What is he doing?
- How did he get there?

We, as scriptwriters, must know these answers in 100% of the cases, although there are some that we do not make known to the viewer. We have to be aware of all the possible directions that our story can take for two reasons: the first is that it is the only way to keep the story under control at all times, preventing it from getting out of hand, and not knowing how to solve the conflict. The second is that only then can we always be one step ahead of the viewer and we will be able to take him where it seems most convenient at any time, since he will become predictable for us.

It is important that these questions appear because they are the ones that will give us the guideline that we are going down a path that is at least interesting. The strong and complex characters are the ones who unleash the most questions, provoke more interest in the viewer, and feed a large number of small successive conflicts, which are those that give fluidity to the story.

Remember that these questions should *always* arise at the beginning of the story. As you progress, new ones will appear, but the initial ones must be present within the first ten minutes. In this way, we will avoid that the viewer falls asleep or leaves the movie theatre, taking advantage of the fact that there is another film that begins at the same time and perhaps he can manage to sneak into it.

68. Recreation: A good chocolate cake with a banana smoothie

If we manage to build interesting characters, unleash a fair amount of questions, and lead to various conflicts, we are likely to sit in front of the computer for long hours that will seem like minutes; and we forget to eat, to sleep, and even to breathe. But the truth is that our brain needs to rest from time to time and surely, we will realize this much later than we should.

To avoid having to erase several pages, full of tired words, it is highly recommended that you learn to listen to your body and change activity at least for ten minutes, maximum every four hours.

Now, pay attention to a small detail that will help you not to go crazy: *under no circumstances reread what you have written when you are tired*; everything will seem like a sum of improbable errors, lacking in structure. As a good screenwriter, you should know that the first version of your script is written with the heart, and the second, with the head. But you will not be able to correct anything with a dysfunctional brain.

The first time you have to turn to this resource –because that's what this point is: a *resource*– will be approximately between the first 15 and 20 minutes of the script. You have already introduced your main characters, unleashed the important conflict, perhaps introduced some secondary ones as well, and are ready to move on with the story. But it is not good to start the second stage tired. Disperse a little. Do not be afraid that your inspiration will go to the neighbor's house, offended by your sudden neglect. It will return when you are calmer, rested and perceptible.

I don't know how to go forward with the story

69. Small successive conflicts

Do you remember when the example of chess was mentioned here? At that time, it was explained that, in order to reach the opposite king, it is necessary to organize different small strategies that will remove the pieces one by one. We cannot simply pretend that the king falls after three moves (except in the case of fool's mate), because we won't be taking advantage of all the tools and secrets you already know cinema has. If you pay attention to movies, you will see that there are tools that are used to change the subject subtly. For example, a cell phone that rings just as two characters finish speaking, a third person who appears in the scene talking about anything else, someone who *remembers* another and muses, '*I wonder what Anne is doing now*'. Or just looks at his watch and says, '*How strange... Anne should be here by now...*'. Any of these comments makes the viewer also remember that momentarily forgotten character, and become interested in his whereabouts, activity, etc. If at that moment, we change the scene and show Anne, the viewer will be satisfied because we have given him what he wanted. This is one of the most subtle ways to move forward in the story from several different points of view. Small successive conflicts do not have to have a necessary direct relationship to the main conflict. Of course, they will progressively lead to it, but moving a bishop to a certain square will not necessarily imply that in the next move we will checkmate the king. As in chess, when writing a script, we can place conflicts that are misleading, that lead the story through longer and cumbersome but more interesting paths, and we can even leave aside for a while -yes, yes... *for a while*- the main conflict to develop some secondary ones that will later relate to it.

The most important thing to know is that small conflicts *give fluidity to the story*; so, it is important that from the beginning you open the game showing at least four or five different issues that will progressively develop. It may be that the viewer does not find any relation with them at first, but he will ask himself what they have to do with one another, so you *must* know, from the beginning, how they connect.

70. The 15-minute crisis

You are turning to this part of the book because you think you have been betrayed. Yes, sir. You were told that inspiration was not going to the neighbor's house, but it is exactly what you are feeling now. You did your homework well, introducing the characters and the main conflict, and took a break, although you did not really feel the need to rest until you sat at the kitchen table and felt the lovely aroma of fresh coffee, and now, determined to continue the work you left behind, you find yourself in the midst of an uncontrolled crisis, wanting to burn the book, because you feel you should have continued with the story when you had inspiration on your side. But do not fear, my friend. There is a solution.

Now that you are as cool as a cucumber again, it is the ideal time to *reread* what you wrote. Once you are done, you will realize that the time for *submission* has passed and you are now facing the *start up*. You feel you do not know where to go because you have *too many choices*. Well, one of the best ways to face this new stage is *delimiting*. How does one do that? Think about how you want your story to end. It is not necessary to imagine the whole scene, but simply the resolution. Is the crime resolved? Is the murderer discovered? Those two who are going to fall in love very soon, do they end up together? Is that strange creature coming from another planet? We will establish the answer you give as our first boundary in the story, whether it is yes or no. Notice how.

If your answer was *'yes,'* our whole story must go the *'no' way, and vice versa*. Keeping in mind how we are going to finish the story, we may not know where to go, but we will know perfectly well where we *do not* have to go, and that, even if we do not believe it, is a great advance. Small limitations help inspiration to manifest. Then you will see that it has not gone anywhere, but, like you, was resting. Sometimes it costs a little to start again, but once you sit down and ask yourself these questions, it will stretch out and go back to work.

Now... what happens with those cases in which, unfortunately, we still do not know how our story will end? Mmmmhhh... What a problem... well... In these cases, what you should do is take your characters and place them in two *opposite* hypothetical paths and see which one is the most interesting. How are you going to realize this? Because it will be... *the one that unleashes the most questions in your mind!* Remember to write them all down, then look at the list. The path that has more questions is the way to go. Great, right?

71. The 30-minute crisis

A classic. Did you think that you would not encounter any more problems after so many useful secrets had already been revealed to you? Well, you were wrong. The path of writing is a long Via Crucis. Now that you have succeeded in befriending successive small conflicts and your story is progressing much more fluidly than you imagined, once again you feel your mind has been left blank. You already have an average of thirty written sheets and suddenly do not know how to continue with your story.

Dear screenwriter, it may happen that your main conflict *has been resolved* or has suddenly become *very predictable* and you know that you will not be able to stretch it for much longer. This is because, when we take alternative paths, sometimes opposed to the one that leads to the resolution of the conflict, we fear that our story will go anywhere, and the connecting thread will be lost. Consumed by this fear, we decide to return to the safe path and suddenly realize that our story will never become a feature film.

The first thing to do is calm down.

Then, retrace your steps to the point where you took the main road. Once you are there, focus on the end of the story again. Now you will have a plus point:

While it is true that you will have to delete several sheets, at least you will know that *that* was your easy path, and once again you will have found another limitation. Now you know perfectly well where you do *not* have to go because you have lived it.

This is the ideal time for your *secondary characters* to become busybodies. Build scenes in which they meet with the main characters and help them to be those charming friends of life who, with all the good will of their advice, convince your protagonist to take... *the wrong way!*

Revisit your characters' possible decisions and note which of them lead towards the end more quickly; then *discard them*. Take that value that you know you have and face the fear of losing control. If you keep your eye on the ultimate goal, no matter how far you send your characters, they will always find a way to get back on track. Make sure they do it within the five or six final pages; remember that resolution of conflicts is very fast in cinema.

72. The 60-minute crisis

Let's see... Let's see... What do we have here? Ahhh... yes... that... No, no... Don't say anything. It's all clear now. You think your story is complete crap, right? You have already written an hour of film and suddenly realize that you wanted to be so original that nobody will believe your story. The viewer is probably already sleeping (if he did not leave the room), you are never going to get your story made and the whole world hates you. But do not worry, you're just going through a little nervous breakdown. Nothing that can't be solved.

You should know, talented screenwriter, that if you have managed to write an hour of film, we will probably find *something* interesting in it.

First, if you feel that your story is not going to be believed, it has to do with an error that, fortunately, can be easily solved. The plausible is not something that appears in a film as if by magic. The plausible *is constructed*. You must establish the rules of the game at the beginning of the story, and what happens to you now is that you probably forgot to do it. So, what you have to do is see what it is that seems implausible, and if you think it is interesting enough to continue working instead of discarding it, go back to the beginning of the story and *present it as something possible*. How do you do it? Have some character mention it as something that he read in the newspaper, or heard on a newscast, or say he met someone who witnessed it, etc. Your characters, like their conflicts and their scenarios, are *constructions* that start from your brain. Any viewer knows that. So, if one of your characters says, for example, that he was kidnapped by an alien, the viewer will not think '*this is too farfetched...*', he will simply say: '*ok... in this film, beings from other planets will appear.*' The reaction of your characters to situations and conflicts is what builds the plausible. So, there it is. Put some magic lines at the beginning or some nice pictures that show what you are showing now, and your problem will be solved.

Secondly, if you see that the story has taken a course that has nothing to do with the beginning, it is probably because you have removed your gaze from the ultimate goal, and now you find that a secondary character is *much more interesting than the main one.* This is a risk you run when you do not know where you are going with your story. The only solution is to erase the beginning of the script and convert the secondary character in the main one from that point or reread the story until you find the point where you deviated and resume from there in another way. But do not feel unmotivated. All experiences are good. From now on you will know what you do not have to do the next time you type, and it will become easier.

73. Annoying questions (because they force you to check the entire text)

As a screenwriter, you should ask yourself the annoying questions throughout the time you are writing. These questions have nothing to do with those that are unleashed from the characters, their decisions and their actions. These questions are of a *structural* nature. Let us hope that the spectator does not think of it, because if they arise in his mind, we will be in a serious problem, because it will mean that the structural failure is so great that even he has noticed it. These questions are of the following sort:

1. How long has my main character not been on the scene for? (I'm in trouble if the answer is: 'More than 15 pages ago.')
2. How long has my antagonist not appeared on the scene for? (Same answer.)
3. How close is my character to achieving his goal? (Let's hope he still has a good time to go if we are in the middle of the script.)
4. How are my characters expressing themselves when they speak? (If they express themselves in a similar way, let's hope they are at least the same age.)
5. Why does this character talk so much? (You may be able to use better cinematographic resources.)
6. Why am I resorting to this scenario so much? (Maybe it's too common.)

As you can see, it is best to write down these kinds of questions on a poster and stick it on the wall of the bedroom. If it's fluorescent, all the better. It is important that you can see them clearly and ask them all the time. It will save a lot of valuable time, as it will help you maintain a neat and orderly structure.

Remember that talent always accompanies the disciplined. The writing of a feature film, as has been seen previously in this book, has a direct relationship with *memory*. As the story progresses, more and more little balls spin in the air, and it becomes increasingly difficult to master them all. Any aide memoire is *always* welcome. You will have enough tools to enrich your story and you will be able to take new and unexpected paths bravely. The more control you have over your story, the more chance you have of being original; and precisely the original stories are the ones which then become cinema classics.

74. Recreation: A bicycle ride

If you feel that you are living a *déjà vu*, know that it is not the intention of these words. It is preferable to be repetitive than to have to regret a string of perfectly avoidable errors. Recesses are *tools* as useful as any other in cinema and writing and in life! The brain is like a muscle, and it can also fatigue. You may not see it or feel it like any of your other muscles, but after so much work, it will not work the same way it did at the beginning.

It is very important that you respect this, because we do not want to waste a screenwriter as talented as yourself because your brain has wilted, after you managed to write only one story.

Recreation also helps inspiration. You can take advantage of these moments to do some of the things that have been suggested previously here. Take a walk, go into a bar to have a drink and take the opportunity to listen to people's conversations; go through different scenarios to see if there are any that relate to your story, and so on. This way you will at least feel that you are not wasting your time, and at the same time you will be resting. Make friends with free time; it is as useful as the rest of the time.

I don't know how to finish

75. The 90-minute crisis

The first thing these lines will do at the moment is... *congratulate you*! If you managed to reach minute ninety in the writing of a script, it means that you have done a lot of hard work and have managed to apply at least thirty of the secrets mentioned here. It means, moreover, that you had the necessary discipline to overcome your frustrations and continue to write beyond everything. But, well, not everything is rosy, and it may happen that you have one last crisis before the end.

Problems in this instance often have to do with *anxiety*. You have already gone too far, you have already worked on too many conflicts and it seems to you that it is time to wrap up the story. But, unintentionally, your story ended abruptly. And you are not happy, because after so much effort, in the end it seems that the story is a shameless ungrateful who does not know how to recognize all the time you have dedicated to it. But conflicts are solved like this. It can take an hour and fifty-nine minutes to organize it, and only a little minute, barely sixty seconds, to solve it. The good thing about this is that you will not have to erase a lot, maybe three or four pages, if you just want to keep moving forward. Do not worry if you got carried away by anxiety; at this point it is not a serious problem.

If, on the other hand, you feel that you have arrived here but do not know how to finish your story, not because there is no possible end, but because there are too many, the solution is not complicated either. Reread the whole story and you will see that somewhere in it is the end you are looking for. Each end you choose will convey a different message to the viewer. For example, if it ends badly, then the viewer will think *'whatever I do, if something shall not be, it will never be...'*; or if it has a happy ending, he will think: *'I should never give up... if I persevere, I will triumph...'*; etc. There is probably a message you want to convey, and if it has been lost in the story, when you reread your story you will remember it and then you will know how to end it. Do not be discouraged, you have so little left to finish!

76. The Anticlimax

This is just a small gift before ending this part of the book. The anticlimax is, as its name implies, *the opposite* of the climax. The climax is the moment of greatest tension of a film and, of course, is always present at the end.

The whole story is like a spring that is tightening more and more. One thing leads to the other, and then to another, and so on, until there comes a point where there is no way to achieve greater tension. The spring is about to explode, and something must happen that no longer allows a return back; something that gives resolution to the story. That moment is present in almost all films, because as it was already mentioned, the end of a film is 75% of the opinion of the spectators; so, no one wants to risk delivering a weak end.

Now, for this end to be even more interesting, the last cramp that can be given to the spring is the *anticlimax*. The anticlimax implies a simple action, but that results in a much richer end. It consists of making the characters do exactly the opposite of what they are going to do in the climax. For example, if the girl is going to run to the airport to prevent her lover from getting on the plane (climax), the previous scene should show them both in an argument that ends with the boy leaving and with her crying looking out the window (anticlimax). The anticlimax reinforces the climax and leaves a much tastier flavor in the mind of the viewer. And since it is so easy to apply, it is a valuable loss when you do not take advantage of it.

The Commercial vs. The Artistic

77. The commercial is not always a betrayal of art. Making money with talent can bring happiness

Many times, when we come up with an idea and start to see all the possible ways of working on it, we quickly rule out the possibility of doing something commercial. We understand that to be able to make art we need to develop our creativity, but that in no way will we be able to make money with what we do. Or worse, we think that *we should not* make money with what we consider art. Then, we establish two columns and place under one the *commercial* and under the other, the *artistic*. And thanks to this, which is nothing more than a social construction, we end up working for others to be able to have money to do what we like, instead of finding the right balance that makes us make money with our art.

But there are ways to do artwork and reach thousands of viewers. You surely know more than a hundred cases. How, then, can *you* be one of those enlightened ones? The answer is, unfortunately, a little simpler than the practice: what you have to do is *find a balance between what we want to convey and the capacity of our model viewer to understand it.*

But many times, due to the initiative of another *social construction,* we think that the artist should *not reduce himself* to explaining his work; he comes to break with the structures and as he is ahead of his time, the one who wants to understand him, should try hard and the one who cannot, well... a pity.

Many artists have already demonstrated, especially throughout the 20th Century, that it is not necessary for art to be reserved for a few. Not only the works that are inside museums are art, and less when it comes to something like the cinema, which has a great possibility of becoming massive. It is important that you as a scriptwriter understand this, especially since no one is going to suffer the consequences of being misunderstood more than you. The viewer will simply leave the movie theatre cursing and forget about you and the entire film crew within five minutes, but you will be frustrated and feel that your hard work has been in vain. If you make a little effort and study the mentality of the one to whom you want to convey your message, maybe you can establish a link and incidentally you can make a little more money with the work you love so much.

It is a myth that you should lower your work to make it more commercial. A talented scriptwriter as yourself must deal with the responsibility of transmitting a message, and for that you have to take into account the type of receiver you are dealing with in each case. It is one of the hardest and most boring parts of artistic expression but know that you will gain greater satisfaction when your audience recognizes you.

78. The love story does not promise a success; nor does the horror genre promise a failure

Myths in cinema are not only used to tell stories; some are meant to be just annoying. When we face some of these myths, what we find is not a new possibility of expression, but quite the opposite: creative limitations.

Maybe we come up with an idea to make a horror movie and discard it immediately because we think it's not worth the effort, as they're probably going to reject our script anyway. And then we forget, perhaps, the best idea that ever occurred to us, and we occupy our mind with that other not-so-interesting love story, but which will be more likely to even be accepted into a production company. We think that the genre of drama or romantic comedy is going to reach more spectators and force our creativity to fit into the social mold.

But you will have seen that there are excellent films in all genres. And yes, perhaps many of them are beyond the initial expectations of the team that worked, but what is valid is not the great success, but the *willingness to try*.

Each writer has more affinity with one genre than with another. If you feel that you get along better with a horror movie than with an adventure movie, you do not need to worry that you will only be able to develop your talent in bizarre, low budget films. Sit in front of your computer and search for the most commercial movies of your favorite genre. You will notice that there are some characteristics that are common to all of them.

Suppose that indeed, you are a horror fan. As we have seen, the monsters of the good films of the genre are worked on in depth and have more motivations and objectives than a simple chip programmed to kill the innocent girl. By the way, in those films, we also find a wide variety of genre mix. There is a love story, police investigations, some dose of the fantastic genre that makes us doubt the origin of the creature, a few elements of suspense and, why not, moments of comedy.

Unlike the horror films that only try to show blood in industrial quantities, these films establish a *connection* with the spectator. They offer a variety of emotions that not only range from the impression caused by the blood to the fear of the wicked evil monster, but goes from tears to the courage of the hero to save his beloved, passing through impression, intrigue and the surprise jump in the armchair, to the laughter at that mistake that the monster makes, which makes it more real and collaborates with the spectator's identification with it.

Horror masters, like most teachers, manage to make money with their artistic expression. And go ask them if they feel guilty because of their bank account; it will make them laugh so much that maybe they will even offer you a job.

79. Timeless stories are more likely to become classics

Some issues have already been mentioned regarding this point. But we will delve deeper into it, as they have a huge relationship with the possibility of making money through artistic expression.

Timeless stories are the most likely to become classics. This is because, as generations pass, there is always some factor in them that achieves identification with the viewer.

For this to happen, we must take into account the Eternal Themes, which have already been seen in depth here. If we manage to be eloquent enough to tell the story we want, considering the presence of these themes, we will achieve not only a much richer film, but also the possibility of reaching more viewers throughout History. That means we are not only going to make money with what we make in cinema, but it will also touch the viewers' hearts at their homes through VOD. And that, assuming we have managed to sell our script at first, because as we have seen, a good amount of time passes between the original idea and the final product.

Just as it is possible to tell any story through any genre, there is always the possibility of incorporating one of the Eternal Themes into any idea. In this way, even if we are telling a specific fact that occurred at a particular time, we can consider that one of the causes of that fact is a Theme always present in Humanity.

It is a shame that this resource is not used, since it is a great idea, simple to apply, and it also helps us to earn more money with a job that will be arduous and thorny anyway.

80. That script under hire can give you the money to dedicate to that other one you want to write. Love it too.

Usually, at the beginning of our career, we have to send resumes to different producers to be able to make some money, gain experience and achieve recognition. This is by no means a betrayal of art. The writer's profession is difficult to face, and it is even more difficult to preserve. We know that we are talented and that every minute that we do not dedicate to creative development is a waste of time. And what we usually think is that if we work on another's idea, we are not being creative. But the artist makes art of everything he touches, that's why he is called *artist*.

Probably the one who hired us to write a script is only thinking about making money and does not care if you are an artist or not. But you should not let that attitude disillusion you. At the very least, you will know that you will get at least a positive thing from it: money. And with that money you can do what you want, even if you invest in filming an idea which is entirely yours that ends up being a resounding failure. Although... that sounds even more demotivating, doesn't it?

Probably what you will end up thinking is that in the end everything is part of a great injustice. *'If I do the work of another, I make money, but I don't do what I want; and if I do what I want, I don't make money.'* Well, you must get that prejudice out of your head and let your talent flow, even if it is to achieve the best script ever written for someone else to take credit for it. At least you will know that you have done your best, beyond any circumstance. *That* is the mentality that makes artists grow.

Anyway, if you still are not convinced, think of it this way: there are people who want to dedicate themselves to writing and in order to achieve it, they must spend their days in an office, working on something for someone which has nothing to do with their profession. Think at least that you are collecting money to write what you want, doing something that, incidentally, can keep you exercising your talent. It will always be preferable to write for another, than to do something that distances you even more from the artistic world that you know you belong to.

Love everything you write. Feel the flow of your gift in every word and, in a short time, you will realize that a great artist is not such because he has the luck to work in what he loves, but because he loves everything in what he works.

Recommended Bibliography

- '*The Story*' by Robert McKee.
- '*Script Model and Models of Scripts*', by Francis Vanoye.
- '*Introduction to Fantastic Literature*', by Tzvetan Todorov.
- '*Hitchcock*', by François Truffaut.
- '*Film Theory*', by Robert Stam.
- '*The Definitive Guide to Screenwriting*', by Syd Field.
- '*Creating Unforgettable Characters*', by Linda Seger.
- '*The Screenwriter's Bible*', by David Trottier.
- '*Save the Cat*', by Blake Snyder.
- '*The Hero's Journey*', by Joseph Campbell.

For any data about any film, you can resort to the website: www.imdb.com (Internet Movie Data Base). From that website another very interesting one derives, called: www.imsdb.com (Internet Movie *Scripts* Data Base). A very extensive source of film scripts. Most in English, but in many other languages too.